P9-BBU-728

CD-art

Innovation in CD Packaging Design

Charlotte Rivers

RotoVision

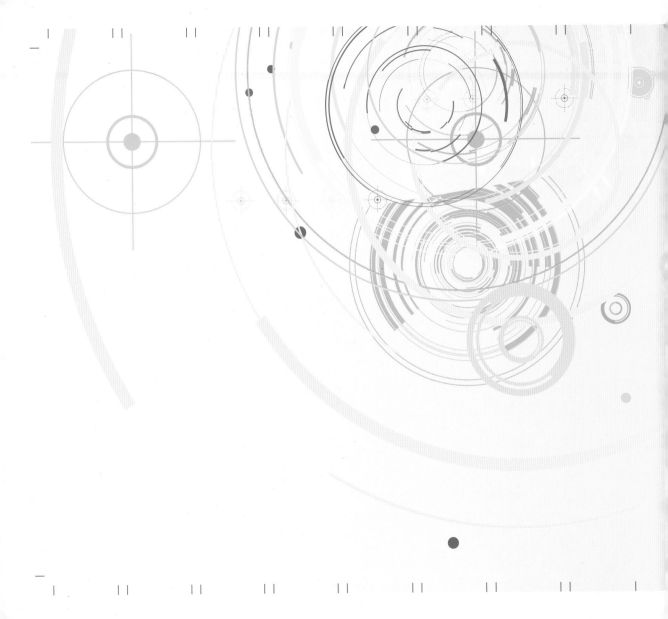

Innovation in CD Packaging Design

Charlotte Rivers

A RotoVision Book
Published and distributed
by RotoVision SA,
Route Suisse 9
CH-1295 Mies, Switzerland

RotoVision SA
Sales and Editorial Office
Sheridan House
114 Western Road
Hove BN3 1DD, UK

Tel: +44 (0)1273 72 72 68
Fax: +44 (0)1273 72 72 69
www.rotovision.com

All rights reserved. No part of this publication may be reproduced,
stored in a retrieval system or transmitted in any form or by any
means, electronic, mechanical, photocopying, recording or
otherwise, without permission of the copyright holder.

While every effort has been made to contact owners of
copyright material produced in this book, we have not always
been successful. In the event of a copyright query, please
contact the Publisher.

10 9 8 7 6 5 4 3 2 1

ISBN: 978-2-88893-013-6

Art Director: Jane Waterhouse
Designer: Simon Slater, www.laki139.com

Reprographics in Singapore by ProVision Pte. Ltd.
Tel: +65 6334 7720
Fax: +65 6334 7721
Printed in China by Midas Printing International Ltd.

Contents

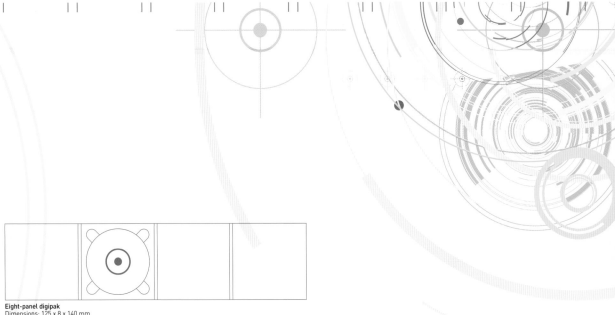

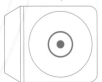

Eight-panel digipak
Dimensions: 125 x 8 x 140 mm
Materials: Card and plastic

Transparent slip case with flap
Dimensions: 129 x 130 mm
Material: Plastic

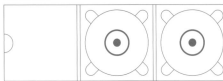

Six-panel double digipak with insert sleeve
Dimensions: 125 x 8 x 140 mm
Materials: Card and plastic

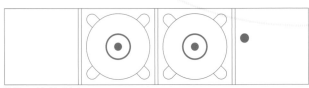

Eight-panel double digipak
Dimensions: 125 x 8 x 140 mm
Materials: Card and plastic

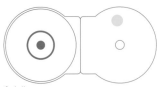

C-shell
Dimensions: 124 x 125 mm
Material: Plastic

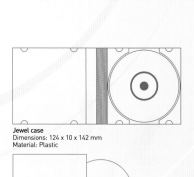

Jewel case
Dimensions: 124 x 10 x 142 mm
Material: Plastic

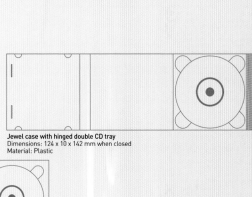

Jewel case with hinged double CD tray
Dimensions: 124 x 10 x 142 mm when closed
Material: Plastic

Slip case
Dimensions: 125 x 125 mm
Material: Card

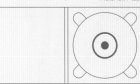

Four-panel digipak
Dimensions: 125 x 8 x 140 mm
Materials: Card and plastic

Eight-panel digipak
Dimensions: 125 x 8 x 140 mm
Materials: Card and plastic

Trigger case (VarioPac)
Dimensions: 143 x 126 mm
Material: Plastic

01

"I've never bought a record without
being influenced by the cover"

Peter Maybury, Peter Maybury Studio

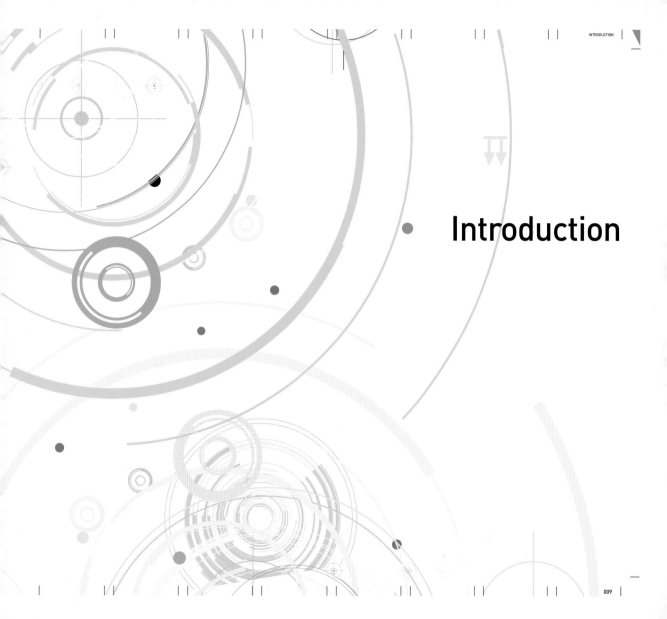

Introduction

Background

An Atlantic Records executive once said, "If the group is big, it don't matter what the cover is. You can wrap it in a brown-paper bag—it makes no difference to sales." The 1979 release of Led Zeppelin's <u>In Through the Out Door</u> was wrapped in exactly that, and sales were more than a little disappointing. Proof, if it were ever needed, that we do judge records much like books—by their covers.

Thankfully not all records were, or are, sold in brown-paper bags. Since 1939, when Alex Steinweiss, then a designer at Columbia Records, suggested replacing standard labels on album covers with original artwork, designers and artists alike have created some of the most stunning and evocative images of the design world.

Album-cover artwork has provided us with some of the finest examples of graphic design in history, and in turn, has launched the careers of some of the greatest, most innovative and influential graphic designers working today. Obvious examples include Peter Saville and Vaughn Oliver, whose work in the 80s and 90s for Factory Records and 4AD respectively, firmly established them as major influences in the long history of album-cover design.

Back in the 50s, the graphic talent of Reid Miles defined jazz music's visual style through his strong typographic covers for the Blue Note label. In the 60s and 70s, art director Gary Burden and photographer Henry Diltz created classic album covers for, among others, The Doors and Joni Mitchell. More recently design companies such as Farrow Design, Stylorouge, Segura Inc., Tomato, Intro, and The Designers Republic have broken new ground in record-sleeve design with work that has gone on to influence graphic design beyond the world of music.

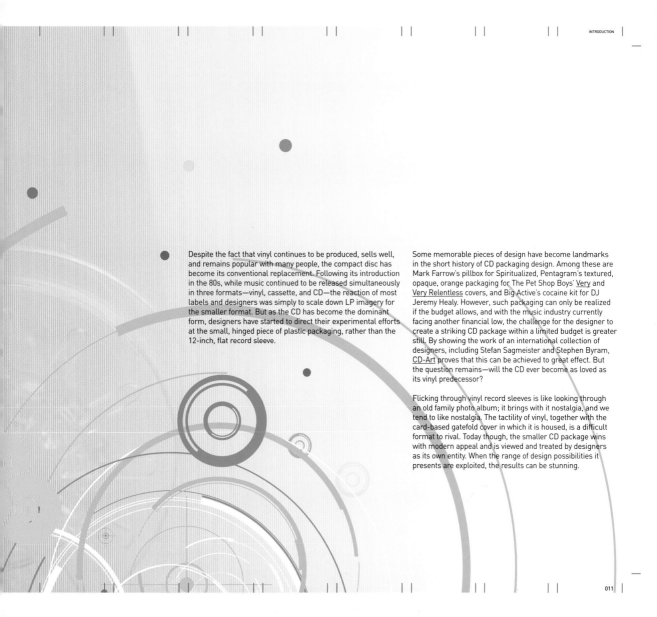

Despite the fact that vinyl continues to be produced, sells well, and remains popular with many people, the compact disc has become its conventional replacement. Following its introduction in the 80s, while music continued to be released simultaneously in three formats—vinyl, cassette, and CD—the reaction of most labels and designers was simply to scale down LP imagery for the smaller format. But as the CD has become the dominant form, designers have started to direct their experimental efforts at the small, hinged piece of plastic packaging, rather than the 12-inch, flat record sleeve.

Some memorable pieces of design have become landmarks in the short history of CD packaging design. Among these are Mark Farrow's pillbox for Spiritualized, Pentagram's textured, opaque, orange packaging for The Pet Shop Boys' Very and Very Relentless covers, and Big Active's cocaine kit for DJ Jeremy Healy. However, such packaging can only be realized if the budget allows, and with the music industry currently facing another financial low, the challenge for the designer to create a striking CD package within a limited budget is greater still. By showing the work of an international collection of designers, including Stefan Sagmeister and Stephen Byram, CD-Art proves that this can be achieved to great effect. But the question remains—will the CD ever become as loved as its vinyl predecessor?

Flicking through vinyl record sleeves is like looking through an old family photo album; it brings with it nostalgia, and we tend to like nostalgia. The tactility of vinyl, together with the card-based gatefold cover in which it is housed, is a difficult format to rival. Today though, the smaller CD package wins with modern appeal and is viewed and treated by designers as its own entity. When the range of design possibilities it presents are exploited, the results can be stunning.

Digital Considerations

Since I wrote CD-Art in 2002, the way we choose, buy, and listen to music has changed dramatically—downloading is now the main way to obtain new music. This is in stark contrast to declining CD sales, which have dropped significantly.

As a consequence, designers have to work harder to encourage people to buy physical music on CD, or, alternatively, look at the design opportunities that the new digital format provides. Recently, designers and labels have experimented with several new ideas in a bid to encourage music lovers to actually purchase music physically rather than digitally. There has been the release of Keane's single, Nothing in My Way, on a memory stick packaged in CD-sized artwork by Big Active, and Beck's do-it-yourself album cover, which also includes a DVD featuring music videos for each track (this got it banned from the official UK charts for having an unfair sales advantage over other albums). There has even been the release of The Blank Album by Superthriller, which is exactly that—a blank CD released by the band's label Rough Trade. The idea is to involve the consumer completely in the process and allow them to master their own album. Once purchased, the CD is taken home, inserted into a computer, and used, together with instructions and tracks on the band's homepage, to create a unique, customized album. All three release ideas are certainly different—they are experimental, risky, and show that the music industry and the designers working in it are willing to try out something new.

Big Active's latest offering, Beck's do-it-yourself cover for his album The Information, which was designed by Gerard Saint together with Mat Maitland and Beck, won a D&AD award. It was an ambitious project, not least because it involved commissioning 20 different artists to create imagery that was used on sheets of stickers, but the result is inspired. "We attempted to create a highly ambitious work reflective of Beck's idiosyncratic and creative approach to his art," explains Saint. "It invites the listener to get involved and participate visually in the album experience. In my opinion that's good design that delivers."

Design: **Big Active**
Album Title: **The Information**
Artist: **Beck**

When Beck's fans buy the album, they also get a booklet of blank graph paper and a sheet of stickers, with which they can create their own album-cover artwork. There is a website onto which they can upload their designs, and one of these designs will be featured on the second pressing of the album. "The plan is to choose a design for the 'for life of' version of the album," explains Saint.

Of course, for big bands signed to major labels, budget is not such an issue, but for indie bands on smaller labels, there is often a limited budget forcing graphic designers to engage in some creative enterprise to make memorable packaging. One such example is a cover created by David Lane for a promo single by the band Gossip. Faced with a minimal budget, Lane used card sleeves and tape to create innovative and great lo-fi packaging.

"I wanted to make the promos stand out as objects and give them something that made them different from the crowd, but, in short, there wasn't much money for the project," explains Lane. "Instead I used tape and simple card sleeves to create the covers... It is rare to have a mass product in design that allows some creative freedom, but at least the music industry is vaguely creative and understands art."

Design: **David Lane**
Single Title: **Standing in the Way of Control**
Artist: **Gossip**

In general, CD packaging is one area in which designers really push the boundaries, often making the packaging as much of a must-have as the product inside, and leading the way in terms of innovation. Not all CD packages are designed within the standard shape and size, and if brief and budgets permit, designers have the opportunity to create almost anything. For the release of Rinôçérôse's Music Kills Me album, David Calderley, at Graphic Therapy, created a package with the CD placed in a circular, gloss black plastic inner case, and then into a black rubber pouch with a sticker. The latest Badly Drawn Boy CD and DVD album Born in the UK has been packaged in a British passport–style cover with two discs sitting on the inside front and back covers, track listings and lyrics on the inside pages, and even a photo and personal details page of Badly Drawn Boy himself, Damon Gough. For the recent release of Self Defence, an album by Unkle, 2manydesigners created a large, fold-up pink box package that features artwork by Futura, and similarly, for the rerelease of Unkle's second album, Never, Never, Land, it created a miniature pizza box with foam studs in which to hold the CDs.

With increasing download sales and decreasing CD sales, can such approaches to packaging design actually encourage people to buy physical rather than digital copies? Cedric Murac, designer at WA75, Paris, summed up his thoughts on how designers should approach CD design. "We should not design disc packaging as a 'cover,' but instead as a 'box' in which sits material that supports the work of an artist. This box has several faces, both inside and out, and the goal is not simply to make a beautiful image / cover to seduce the consumer, it is also to support the artists and give them a strong presence. Yes, we have to make smaller images, but nothing obliges us to remain in the jewel case."

Or as Saint of Big Active points out, "Music needs to be sold in a similar way to books, with appropriate 'softback' and 'hardback' versions available. I believe this is a really good way of looking at the idea of digital downloads and actual physical product— each can deliver different aspects of a release and these can be best suited to the characteristic traits of each medium." He adds, "Design is more than just superficial decoration—it's about ideas and problem-solving," Saint continues, "and this is just as relevant with music packaging as it is with designing for any other product. I think our solution for the new Beck album is very much a good example of the difference design can make. The packaging cannot be divorced from the physical format— it is integral to it. It's about getting people inspired."

Design: Non-Format
Album Title: 28 After
Artist: Black Devil Disco
               Club

It was with this thought in mind that examples of CD packaging were chosen for inclusion in this book, which showcases work from more experimental designers who continue to challenge the conventions of music packaging. Inevitably, much of the work featured is from designers working for musicians outside the commercial mainstream, on smaller labels, from musical genres such as lounge, hip hop, jazz, and dance. For the most part, this area of the music industry allows designers more freedom, trusting them to interpret the music visually, and support the artist in the way they believe to be most appropriate. There are few rules, regulations, or guidelines to follow here.

Whether working for a mainstream or an independent label, CD packaging provides designers with the same opportunity. First, as one might expect with any packaging project, there is the chance to tackle a product design problem: how is the pack fabricated? How does it open and close? And unlike many other packaging briefs, there is often an opportunity for editorial design in the inserted booklets, for the art direction of photography other than of the product itself, and so on. In other words, there is scope for experimentation in both two and three dimensions. Consequently, this book has been divided into two main areas of focus: Form looks at the physical characteristics of CD packaging, while Content explores the two-dimensional artwork contained inside.

Firstly Form. This chapter explores the shape, size, and tactility of the CD cover. It is an area of CD packaging in which designers and manufacturers are, increasingly, finding alternatives to the traditional jewel case. Examples range from the extreme—the Sandpaper Blues album that accompanied a London art exhibition of the same name, which had a sandpaper cover—to the sublime. The organic shape of Marc Newson's alternative doughnut CD case is one example.

Secondly, the extensive Content chapter looks at photography, mixed media, and illustration within album-cover design, showing that many designers opt for creative imagery as opposed to uninspiring, vacuous band shots. The bulk of the artwork and text in a CD package is, of course, inside the casing, and not seen by the consumer until they have bought the package. After size, this is one of the most significant differences between vinyl and CDs. The information is hidden, meaning the exterior imagery has to be enigmatic in order to encourage the consumer to become curious about the interior. The CD package does not have to be immediately legible. Indeed, figuring out the mysterious runic inscriptions is part of the pleasure of examining music packaging. Examples here show how designers approach readability in a variety of ways.

Design: **No Days Off**
Album Title: **Crazy Itch Radio**
Artist: **Basement Jaxx**

Popular music is, arguably, the main area of cultural production that people most closely identify with events or periods in their lives, and which they feel "belongs" to them. And album cover art is one of the few areas of graphic design that the public at large actually takes notice of or has an interest in. The combination of this interest and the experimental, often irreverent, and sometimes controversial nature of many album covers has meant that they have become defining cultural objects. The great album covers of the past—Peter Blake's Sergeant Pepper's, Andy Warhol's The Velvet Underground & Nico—are icons familiar to millions who could not describe a single book jacket, much less an annual report or brochure.

Today, several factors contribute to what some perceive as a growing homogenization of album-cover design, not least the strict management by record labels of every aspect of a band's visual identity, as though they were a corporate brand, which discourages risk-taking. Cover art on mainstream pop releases is largely a market-driven affair—retouched, polished pictures of the artist, bold type, and a nonthreatening layout. Why? Well, from a marketing point of view, album-cover art has to perform two essential functions to entice the browsing consumer to pick the album up, study it more closely, and buy it; and to be a creative visual representation of the music inside. On top of the record company's agenda, bands often have clear ideas about how they want their album cover to look. Dialogue on such jobs typically goes through the artist, management, and the label's marketing department before the art director of the cover gets any input. For the designer, major labels can prove to be more of a challenge because commercial viability and unit cost are major issues for consideration, and at times may lead to heavy compromise.

The major labels are becoming increasingly concerned with branding and conforming to convention, rather than experimenting and pushing creative boundaries. Over the past 15 years, the music industry has grown so substantially that there is now extremely heavy competition for high chart positions, with an unprecedented number of releases every week. This has, in turn, led to the creation of record label marketing departments who inform and influence much of the design we see today, and to a saturated market in which many great designs are swallowed up and go unnoticed.

Design: **Airside / Mika / Da Wack**

Album Title: **Life in Cartoon Motion**

Artist: **Mika**

<u>Wire</u> magazine editor Rob Young compares the difference between the independents and the major labels. "Indies tend to work more closely with the artists themselves, while majors are, by definition, such large entities that the visual presentation is often the result of marketing meetings, in-house designers, etc. The artist supplies the recording, but the company—which is there to generate capital above all—engineers the sellable unit rather like a production line." He continues, "Small independent labels are more likely to have been set up by people who are in it primarily for the music, and their businesses will not have anything like the same infrastructure of a major label. So they are working more closely with the artist, and may even have been set up specifically to release the music of a certain artist, so there is more care taken in the visual aspects too. Generally there seems to be more willingness in that sector to treat the record release as a total entity, rather than just a music unit with a wrapping. The independents are more likely to perceive that the wrapping can actually contain a vital and significant part of the artist's vision."

Thus, there are labels—typically the independents—willing to push the boundaries when it comes to creating artwork and packaging. The design process differs in that the dialogue usually takes place directly between artist and designer. This allows for freedom of ideas and the creation of covers that reflect the music rather than present a vacuous marketable image of an artist or band.

Practical considerations such as protection and storage are just as important as aesthetics. The difficult-to-open and easy-to-break jewel case remains the standard CD packaging option. Its use is not necessarily favored by designers, but it is usually required either to remain within budget or to satisfy the larger record labels who tend to have an aversion to anything else. However, as work throughout this book shows, this has not stopped designers from experimenting within the constraints of the jewel-case format. Whether it be having them produced in solid or transparent colors, omitting the booklet altogether to take full advantage of its clear, minimalist aesthetic, or housing it in a variety of slipcases and end cards, the simple changes help set these examples apart from the average CD package.

Design:
Album Title:

Artist:

Non-Format
I Dreamt
Constellations Sang
Motohiro Nakashima

The digipak, in all its various formats, continues to be a popular and practical replacement for the jewel case. The one-piece card-stock case with an attached plastic CD tray closely replicates the gatefold LP, is more environmentally friendly, and is a far more flexible format to work with than the jewel case. The tray in which the disc sits is available in a variety of colors and can be placed in the center, or to the left or right. It can fold out into anything from four to ten panels in various combinations, and die-cut slots or pockets allow for the inclusion of booklets.

This flexibility gives the art director the opportunity to create a design as a three-dimensional piece of art. The long, wraparound format of a six-panel digipak allows for continuous panoramic imagery to be applied to the cover, for example Rik Bas Backer's work for A.P.C. (p95 and p124), or continuous type, as used by Work in Progress on Fischerspooner's album (p116).

Although the digipak is currently the most popular CD-packaging format, packaging companies and graphic designers are constantly developing alternatives. A move away from plastic to materials such as uncoated card or Tyvek® adds to the tactile experience of the consumer (see Materials pp44–61) as well as differentiating the artist's album from its plastic counterparts. With uncoated card, the tactility of such materials can conjure up notions of authenticity. The digifile is another cost-effective alternative. It is the same format as the digipak from card, using die-cut slots for the disc and booklet instead of plastic trays. Packaging like the eco-wallet and Ecopak® provide the environmentally conscious designer or artist with a packaging option that is both practical and responsible. The relatively new use of Tyvek® covers could prove increasingly popular, as tests have shown that the material provides a higher level of disc protection than any other sleeve system available.

So what does the future hold for the music industry? And what can designers and record labels do to move with the "digital times?" As US designer Neal Ashby of Ashby Design points out, "While I believe there will always be a certain market for physical music packaging, especially within fringe and niche markets, the concept of music packaging as we know it is definitely on the precipice of a new era in design. The fact that audiences today have the ability to control their music experiences far more than even 15 years ago presents both challenges and opportunities for today's designers, and calls upon them to further consider the implications of their choices.

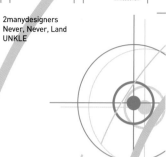

Design: 2manydesigners
Album Title: Never, Never, Land
Artist: UNKLE

Computer Arts Projects editor Dom Hall agrees. "I think it's fair to say that the golden age of music packaging is over, and while it's a crying shame that the generation starting to discover the joys of pop music now will never experience the thrill of seeing a new Malcolm Garret, Vaughn Oliver, or Designers Republic cover on the shelves of their local record shop, and spend ages pouring over all of the images and tiny hidden details great covers have, the design industry is nothing if not inventive and resourceful and I feel confident that there are lots of brilliant alternatives just waiting to be developed."

For example, an interview featured with George White, Senior Vice President of Strategy and Product Development at Warner Music Group, revealed that quite a lot can be done. His team at Warner has been working to develop something it calls iLiner or interactive liner note. As he explains, "It combines all the elements you would find in traditional album artwork into an interactive presentation that launches right in iTunes... We've done them for 15 different albums and gotten a very positive response from consumers."

An example of a similar project is something that Warner did for Gnarls Barkley—it took the liner notes and created a "fly-through," moving the viewer through the lyrics and artwork associated with the album on their iPod, but allowing them to use the scroll wheel to move backward and forward through this experience. Increasingly, labels are approaching the physical and digital aspects in a more combined and integrated manner, as Chris Murphy of Fällt does with his sub-label Fodder. Music on Fodder is released digitally, the virtual singles have A and B sides and come with easy-to-download, print, and assemble "sleeves" in a PDF format.

All that said, one hopes that, even in the face of such technological advances, consumers will still want to purchase the CD package, even if they can download the same music from the Internet onto an MP3 player; that they will still want the whole experience of opening up a package and listening to a new album while flicking through a booklet of words and imagery. As well as fixing the music in the mind of the public visually and aurally, the album cover provides designers with a widely disseminated platform on which to display their ideas to an enormous, diverse, and, most importantly, genuinely passionate audience. It has been a field of great experimentation over the years, providing designers with a creative platform unhindered by many of the corporate constraints that impinge on freedom and creativity in other areas of graphic design. But more importantly, album covers provide music history with a visual archive and become markers of eras. To allow the MP3 file to spell the end of this would be doing an injustice to the visual expression of a valuable notion: the here and now.

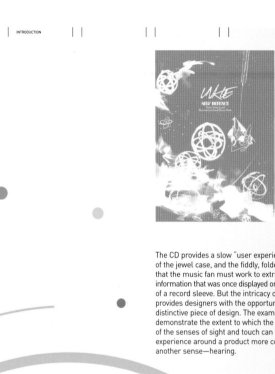

Design: **2manydesigners**
Album Title: **Self Defence**
Artist: **UNKLE**

The CD provides a slow "user experience." The tight clasp
of the jewel case, and the fiddly, folded booklet inside, mean
that the music fan must work to extract the imagery and
information that was once displayed on the front and back faces
of a record sleeve. But the intricacy of that packaging itself
provides designers with the opportunity to create a memorable,
distinctive piece of design. The examples shown in this book
demonstrate the extent to which the successful exploitation
of the senses of sight and touch can create a fuller and lasting
experience around a product more commonly associated with
another sense—hearing.

Charlotte Rivers

"Digital packages ... are an exciting start to a new generation of music packaging."

Neal Ashby, Ashby Design

Neal Ashby is Principal of Ashby Design whose clients include Warner Bros. Records, Virgin Entertainment Group, Capitol Records, ESL Records, EMI Music Group, and National Geographic. For 10 years, Neal was Vice President and Creative Director for the Recording Industry Association of America (RIAA). His award-winning work has been published by Print, HOW, I.D., Graphis, and Communication Arts magazines, and displayed at the Rock and Roll Hall of Fame and Museum in Cleveland, Ohio, and the Experience Music Project in Seattle, Washington.

What do you think the future holds for music packaging now that so much music is downloaded?
While I believe that there will always be a certain market for physical music packaging, especially within fringe and niche markets, the concept of music packaging as we know it is definitely on the precipice of a new era in design. Obviously, what we will begin to see is more emphasis on digitized components such as eBooks, guides, and fully scripted rich media elements that complement their corresponding downloaded music. While this is, in part, no doubt attributable to a need for value-added components to compensate for a perceived lack of tangibility associated with downloaded music, they are important steps in the right direction. Such digital packages, while rudimentary by print package standards, are an exciting start to a new generation of music packaging.

How do you think the role of the graphic designer might change because of this?
More than ever, designers will find themselves scripting or directing a dynamic experience for the listener. With new dynamic components that can be coupled or triggered directly from tracks or albums, traditional printed packaging displays an even greater disconnect between the audible and the visual. There becomes a sense of narrative that is arguably much more present than in print media. It will be these new narrative qualities that will give designers the ability to connect their graphic elements closely with specific musical content.

What can designers do to move with the "digital times" and offer buyers something other than simply a thumbnail image of an album cover when they download music?
Because iTunes provides a little square for the cover art of a song doesn't mean that designers should feel content with filling just that space. Designers and software developers need

to work together in developing ways to deliver this new rich media. I believe there is an increasing need for a more flexible, standards-based approach based on technology available to all, rather than a few. This, along with the continued evolution of the Internet and broadband connectivity, will provide a more dynamic experience available on an on-demand level.

Rather than mourning the death of physical music packaging, should we instead celebrate the arrival of a whole new image / music format?
Absolutely. It does no good to look back. Designers must keep pace with every facet of culture and society, regardless of their position.

What interesting downloadable music packaging and online / interactive elements for music releases have caught your eye?
Examples of good interactive design are few and far between. Apple's iTunes has taken steps to include elements in album downloads to increase the value of the purchase and compete with physical counterparts. These eBooks or guides really show that this type of content is possible and that companies are willing to pursue such avenues. What has evolved are specific album-related websites or portals accompanying music releases. What I would like to see is the convergence of these two media into a unified approach to delivering song or album-specific content.

Rob O'Connor, Stylorouge

Rob O'Connor began work as Designer / Art Director at Polydor Records before founding Stylorouge, the design studio of which he is now Creative Director. A keen photographer (his work forms the basis of Stylorouge's own photolibrary) and avid collector of music, his enthusiasm for diversity has earned him a reputation not only as an art director, but also as a film and video director.

What do you think the future holds for music packaging now that so much music is downloaded?

Music is like any art form based on human inspiration and endeavor—it is a blessing and is essentially free. Historically, it was always a form of communication and self-expression; the social aspect of music was crucial, as it still is. However, the only way it could be sold before sheet music arrived was either through performance or by someone (generally very wealthy) commissioning a piece by a recognized composer for an event, a gift, or a religious or state celebration. The process of popularizing music was a natural consequence of consumerism during the 20th century, where the music that people were "given" free on the radio was packaged as a desirable commodity, along with the people who made it (the cult of personality), and sold as a physical product. All consumer industries have had to reinvent themselves in the age of cheap manufacturing and the widespread accessibility offered by the Internet. The music industry had the extra complication of the intangibility of its product. Cars, furniture, and chocolate, for example, can't be delivered virtually. The radio / retail-led music industry was slow to realize the threat the Internet posed to its omnipotence. Some complacent veterans of the late 20th century were even in denial about the new culture, dismissing it as a fad. The age of blockbuster culture in music may well be in sharp decline, and with it, the sales of the artists who have traditionally followed in the slipstream of the acknowledged best-sellers (Elton John, Madonna, Metallica, Eminem). The sales figures of those in the second, third, and fourth divisions of popular music have dropped markedly, whereas the specialist niche markets have picked up, often kick-starting careers that the old order would have snuffed out at the start, or resurrecting sales of long-dead albums and singles. These new specialist markets, and the music-makers who are using the Internet to inspire their own "do-it-yourself" business are presenting new marketing propositions; albeit with less money, little experience, and often without a discernible market to sell to. But those who are more resourceful and energetic are proving able to succeed, on a small scale, without incurring the costs of the traditional store-led music industry, and not slavishly copying the marketing strategies that have traditionally been employed by the majors for years. The fast turnaround of the modern music business, its transience, and its reliance on television (in particular reality TV) has created a multitude of short careers, and diminished the respect for music in general. The retail price of CDs has dropped drastically in an attempt to win back the market that has been tempted toward file-sharing websites, and this in turn has created a perception of lower value for music. In effect, it has almost become free again. Only a draconian legal regime to fight piracy and the inventiveness of new legal delivery initiatives will turn the industry around. One of the consequences of the download era has been the loss of contextual visual material at its most basic—the record sleeve. Although sadly less ubiquitous than in the golden years of the 70s, 80s, and 90s, the sleeve survives—just. But there is still the need to create other visual material to announce the availability of a new release, or as an accompaniment to enhance the listener's musical experience. The other areas in which imagery still thrives are: the print marketing campaign (posters, press ads, etc); online marketing; video (promo clips, live footage, interview-based advertorials, documentaries, etc; TV advertising; merchandise and promotional material; web design (including MySpace, etc); and tour advertising.

"One of the consequences of the download era has been the loss of contextual visual material at its most basic—the record sleeve."

How do you think the role of the graphic designer might change because of this?
Designers will have to embrace these other creative areas and practice the skills that they demand.

What can designers do to move with the "digital times" and offer buyers something other than simply a thumbnail image of an album cover when they download music?
It is the suppliers of downloadable music who will dictate the "value-added" visual content that will attract the consumer to buy more than just the occasional favorite track. A beautifully designed and functional interface-based experience, such as that proposed by Warner Music in the US, would be an incentive. Added content such as video and extra still imagery would also become the norm. Also, musical artists are already considering abandoning the physical album as a medium, preferring instead to include financial and other incentives to get people to buy a complete body of work via download. I believe Radiohead is one such band. With its already demonstrated love of the book format, I can imagine it offering a bonus along these lines as an incentive. As outrageous as it may seem, I can also imagine more artists considering a return to the concept album—a collection of related material that would be seen as "greater than the sum of its parts."

Rather than mourning the death of physical music packaging, should we instead celebrate the arrival of a whole new image / music format?
The way music is consumed is bound to change—the important thing is for all parties to communicate with each other to explore possible solutions for the common good, and this should be aimed more at creative excellence and not just profit.

02

"Jewel cases are an incredible phenomenon of bad design in form, function, handling, storing, material, and tactile quality on a huge scale. I cannot believe they're still used in ways other than irony"

Christof Steinmann, Spezialmaterial

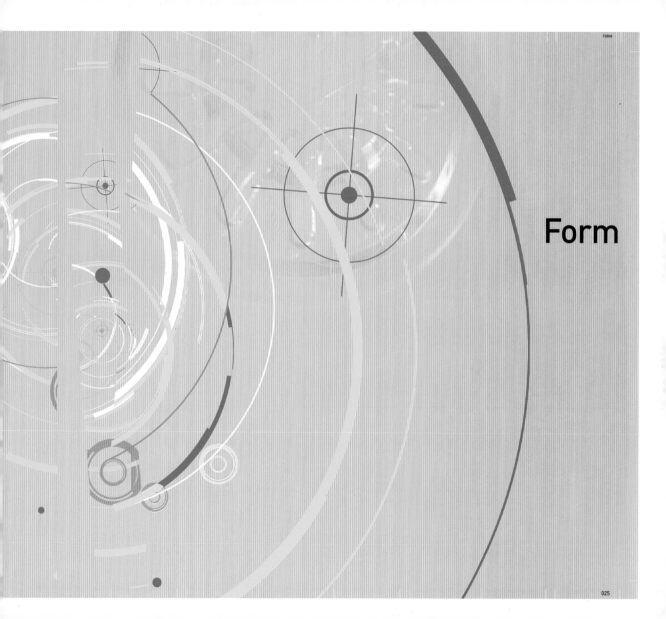

Form

> "I don't think there is any other item or product that offers so many design possibilities as the CD"

Stefan Alt, Salt

Introduction

When the 12-inch square vinyl cover shrank to the 5 x 5½-inch square CD format a certain aesthetic was lost along the way. For the consumer, flicking through a row of CDs was somehow not as pleasing as going through a stack of vinyl. For the designer, it was a case of adapting to completely different dimensions and design requirements. This change of format signalled a fresh approach to album artwork and designers have since attempted to maximize the wealth of new design opportunities available.

Although the difficult-to-open and easy-to-break clear plastic jewel case is the standard format for CD packaging, designers and manufacturers are becoming more inventive. They're discovering various ways to differentiate it as well as developing alternative packaging formats. The use of O cards, belly-bands, screw fastenings, die-cutting, embossing, alternative materials, solid color jewel cases, and so on means that the standard size format can be maintained, without sacrificing originality. These jewel cases give increasing control over the feel and appearance of the packaging.

Choosing the material in which to house a music disc is central to the design. The tactile nature of the CD casing remains in the memory just as the artwork on the cover fixes it visually in the mind. The impression given by the feel is as important as the look, and together these elements engineer the experience. Designer Steven Byram rarely works within the constraints of the jewel case. Instead he uses uncoated card as favored by Japanese retailers Muji.The material brings quality and honesty to any package or product in the same way one assumes a package made of a thick, textured stock with silver foil-blocked type is of high quality. This, rightly or wrongly, means that

the unexpected feel of a CD package can create an impression of quality or truth, but more importantly interest, making it distinctive and memorable for the viewer.

If the budget allows, unusual shapes and sizes can be explored. Artomatic's packaging for the limited-edition release of Alexander McQueen's CD (p71) demonstrates how the CD package can be made into a highly desirable and collectable item. Similarly, but on a smaller budget, Spezialmaterial (p45 and p148) is known for its close attention to detail and innovation in its packaging; using wood, hand-stitching, and even modified potato chip packets! That said, practicality often rules over outlandish, costly, or labor-intensive design, and most CDs remain in a jewel case. However, simple paper manipulation—embossing or die-cutting—or the use of solid-color jewel cases are other ways in which designers can be innovative within the usual constraints. The key is attention to detail, and considering how the user will interact with the package; this adds another dimension and gives that all-important reason to want to own it.

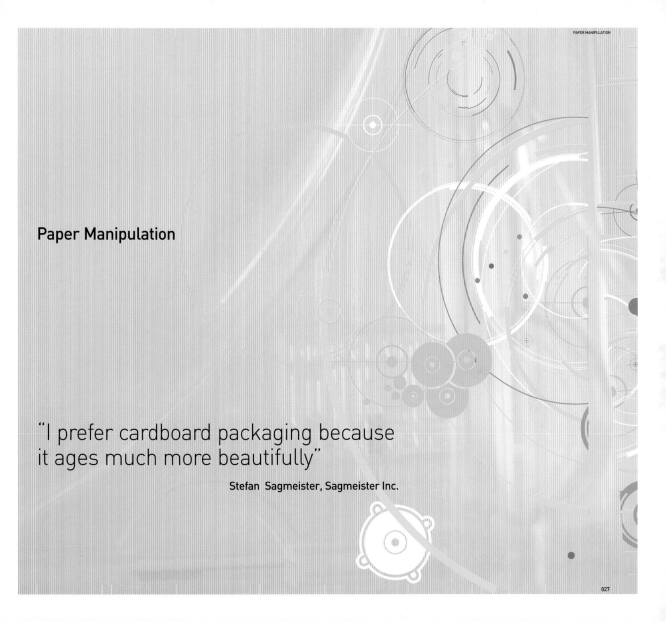

Paper Manipulation

"I prefer cardboard packaging because
it ages much more beautifully"

Stefan Sagmeister, Sagmeister Inc.

Artist:	**Boom Bip**
Label:	**Lex**
Sleeve Artist:	**ehquestionmark, UK**
Effect:	**Foil-blocked, die-cut uncoated card**

Seed to Sun

Lex is a sub-label of UK record label Warp Records. This release by artists Boom Bip is described as being a mellow and soothing listening experience comparable to having a warm drink— at least that was the thinking behind the design. The sleeve was created by ehquestionmark, who made around 300 coffee-mug ring stains, then chose 12, one for each track, and merged them to make the cover artwork.

A typeface was designed for the inner sleeve that houses the CD, based on the CD's barcode. This was applied full bleed to the exterior of the sleeve. The package is made from 400gsm brown-lined, chip-card stock, with Midnight Satin foil-blocked text, and a die-cut hole in the back to reveal the barcode on the inner sleeve.

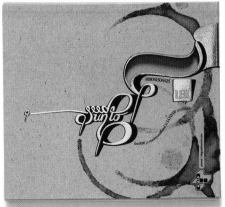

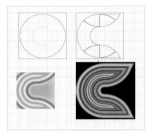

Artist: Lemon Jelly
Label: XL and Impotent Fury
Design: Fred Deakin for Airside, UK
Illustration: Fred Deakin for Airside
Effect: Intricate die-cuts

Spacewalk

Fred Deakin is a director at design agency Airside, and is also part of the band Lemon Jelly, for whom his company designs all its single and album covers. Deakin's dual role makes things easier in terms of briefs and ideas, allowing for greater experimentation.

This intricate die-cut single sleeve, which draws strongly on patterns and flat color (see also p91), reflects the general identity of Lemon Jelly. At first glance this package appears empty, even when the inner wallet is removed. This is because die-cut holes in the sleeve only show the transparent edge of the 5-inch CD, as the CD only has data printed across a diameter of 3 inches.

The sleeve is text-free as with all Lemon Jelly releases. However, for in-store recognition the covers are shrink-wrapped and have a sticker on them containing the album title, some track details, and so on. The package was expensive to produce, but capitalized on Lemon Jelly fans' appreciation of the band's unique flair for packaging design.

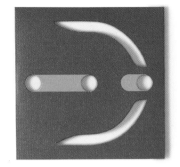

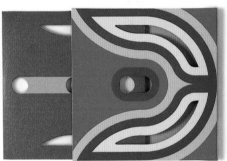

DANIEL BEDINGFIELD GOTTA GET THRU THIS

ALBUM SAMPLER

Artist: Daniel Bedingfield
Label: Polydor Records
Design: Michael Nash Associates, UK
Effect: Typographic die-cuts

Gotta Get Thru This

This is the promotional version of Gotta Get Thru This, a mix of R&B and garage, which gave UK artist Daniel Bedingfield his first number one. Michael Nash Associates created this cover for the release, by using a simple, bold typeface, Brassplate, die-cutting it on the front, and using silk-screen printing on the back. The outer white sleeve and inner fluorescent orange sleeve are made from standard, single-sided, record sleeve card.

Artist: Tosca
Label: G-Stoned
Design: Sarah Littasy for Cuttings, Austria
Photography: Markus Rössle
Effect: Embossed, debossed, and die-cuts

Suzuki

Tosca's Suzuki album and EP are down-tempo electric affairs from one half of Kruder and Dorfmeister, Richard Dorfmeister, and school friend Rupert Huber. Based in Vienna, the pair have been producing and releasing tracks for over seven years and are known for their great attention to detail, not only within the music, but also in their videos and album covers.

Able to invest a little more in production costs, designer Sarah Littasy has used a book format, manufactured by Herzog Idex GmbH, Germany. Embossing, debossing, and spot varnish are used to apply imagery of Huber and Dorfmeister in specially made Tosca dressing gowns on the cover.

Artist:	Jazzanova
Label:	Jazzanova
	Compost Records
Design:	Jutojo, Germany
Photography:	Jutojo
Effect:	Die-cut book

In Between

In Between is the first album from German music collective Jazzanova. Three DJs and three producers make up the group whose influences include jazz, folk, and soul. Berlin-based designers Julie Gayard, Toby Cornish, and Johannes Braun of Jutojo have created a chunky book-like package for the CD using six die-cut pieces of 1mm thick card. These have been cloth-bound and when closed the viewer is presented with a complete image that then breaks down with each turn of the page.

The red line form seen on the cover spells Jazzanova in wire letters, a line-drawn version of which has become the Jazzanova logo. The idea is that it can be changed in a variety of ways: positioning the wire letters at different angles, dangling them, and so on to capitalize on their three-dimensional qualities. This is important, as it is also used for club visuals to accompany the DJs.

Artist:	**TLM**
Label:	**Hydrogen Dukebox Records**
Design:	**Yacht Associates, UK**
Effect:	**Die-cut O card**

Artist:	**Tom & Joyce**
Label:	**Yellow Productions**
Design:	**WA75, France**
Illustration:	**WA75**
Effect:	**Profile die-cuts**

Tom & Joyce

In some cases the artwork for a CD cover is so strong that the designer chooses to omit all text and let the artwork speak for itself. Of course this is neither possible nor appropriate for many releases but for French bossa nova duo Tom & Joyce, designers WA75 felt that a lack of text on the cover could be justified, and instead applied text to a removable belly-band.

"The belly-band was used because we did not want to put the name of the artist on the cover. It was a bit of a challenge to do that with quite an unknown artist, but we thought it would add a little mystery to it," explains cover designer Cedric Maurac. The success of the album proved that this was a good tactic. On the practical side, the belly-band also helps to keep the digipak closed.

The simple yet bold graphic imagery on the cover is intended to act as an identity for the duo, with extensions of the design likely to feature on forthcoming singles and other artwork. The promo version of the album came in a clear plastic sleeve with imagery and text silk-screen printed on both sides.

Electrostars

Yacht Associates received a Best Special Packaging nomination at the Music Week Awards 2002 for the design of this cover. They wanted to create something special but had a limited budget, so took a less-is-more approach to the design; an unprinted disc sits inside a clear jewel case that comes in a plain white, die-cut slip case. Money that would otherwise have been used for artwork and inlays was used to die-cut the octagonal shape, and a series of four CDs—cyan, magenta, yellow, and black—were produced for this commercial release. It shows how effective a simple idea can be and as Chris Thomson of Yacht Associates says, "It challenges record companies who visibly squirm when the words 'special packaging' are mentioned."

Artist:	REM
Label:	Warner Bros.
Design:	Michael Stipe of REM and
	Chris Bilheimer, USA
Illustration:	Michael Stipe
Photography:	Michael Stipe

Reveal (top left and right)
This CD cover is based on record cover dimensions, with a book replacing the vinyl inside. The stencil designs within the book were laser-cut, which explains the precise detail and slight burn marks at the edges. Chris Bilheimer, in-house designer for REM, and band member Michael Stipe, were nominated for a 2001 / 2002 Grammy award for this packaging.

Artist:	REM
Label:	Self-released
Design:	Chris Bilheimer, USA
Illustration:	Chris Bilheimer and
	Michael Stipe
Photography:	Chris Bilheimer and
	Michael Stipe

Christmas promotional pack (left)
This was inspired by another CD package created for Émigré. Designed by Bruce Licher of Independent Project Press and Rudy Vanderlans at Émigré, this was a sleeve that could hold a CD and calendar. The REM packages were assembled by hand and so had to be easy to put together. The gold used to print imagery and text on the uncoated stock is a mix of gold ink and clear varnish.

Artist:	**Various**
Label:	**Universal**
Design:	**Erik Torstensson for Winkreative, UK**
Photography:	**Christopher Griffiths**
Effect:	**Embossed**

Swiss 1

Following the collapse of Switzerland's airline Swissair in October 2001, Tyler Brûlé's creative agency Winkreative was asked to create a new brand for its replacement, Swiss. Along with the design of a new identity, staff uniforms, aircraft livery, website, signage and so on, Winkreative also compiled and designed a CD for the airline that Brûlé describes as an audio extension of the new brand.

"The entire branding project stands firmly in the tradition of Swiss graphic design, a factor that was a priority when compiling this CD. As we want every aspect of the airline to have a strong Swiss link, we hired Swiss DJ and journalist Olivier Rohrbach to compile the CD, and he ensured that all four official languages were included while still keeping the mix international," explains Brûlé.

The packaging design is consistent with the whole airline identity: it is modern, clean, and prestigious. Type was screen-printed on to the white jewel case in white ink. The O card was used to add an extra dimension to the packaging as well as to build on one of the values of the airline—that a little extra is very important. It was embossed with the album name and an insert inside folds out into a small poster.

Artist: Brothers in Sound
Label: Regal Recordings
Design: Tony Hung for
Adjective Noun, UK
Effect: Die-cut, embossed

Family is for Sharing (left)
The High and Low Show (right)
Designer Tony Hung of Adjective Noun
has designed most of the covers for Regal
Recording's releases since redesigning
the label in 1999. These sleeves were for
two promo releases by artists Brothers in
Sound, and Hung's brief was to keep the
design consistent with the look of the
label. "The first few promos I designed for
Regal were highly conceptual and pretty
crazy, often an event in their own right,"
explains Hung. "When I thought about
this one I felt that it would be good to
keep the look moving, yet relevant, so I
looked into developing a very strong
graphic and bold color scheme instead."

Hung used a standard CD wallet but
with a die-cut circle in the front for
identification purposes (there is no other
text on the cover) and a series of
embossed grooves on the front and back.
"One of the advantages of using this
packaging is that most (mainstream) CDs
are packed in jewel cases, so packaging
non-mainstream music in non-mainstream
packaging seemed like a good start. In
addition these promos are a very
important piece of identity to a record
label, as they go out to the DJs, radio
stations and so on; therefore they need
to represent the label and their ideals
correctly. I feel the simple use of
embossing communicates Regal's
attention to detail and 'that something
extra' which is in line with its
music output."

Artist: **Various**
Label: **Staalplaat**
Design: **Alorenz, Germany**
Effect: **Blind-embossed,
hand-numbered**

Alva Noto, Signal, Byetone, and Komet

Mort Aux Vaches is a series of albums by various artists released on Staalplaat for which the basic packaging format shown here is always used (see also p63 and p74). For this release, featuring tracks by Alva Noto, Signal, Byetone, and Komet, Angela Lorenz has used the minimal sounds on the album as inspiration for the cover design. In certain lights it appears blank until tilted slightly to reveal the type, set in Akzidenz Grotesk, that has been blind-embossed onto pure white, textured, 400gsm stock. The CD is held in a four-panel folded card cover that is simply held together by a paper binder. Production of the 1000 limited copies of this album was both lengthy and costly, but as with all Mort Aux Vaches releases, attention to detail in the packaging is as important as the music itself.

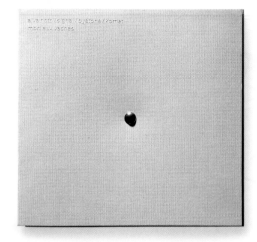

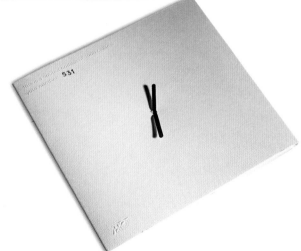

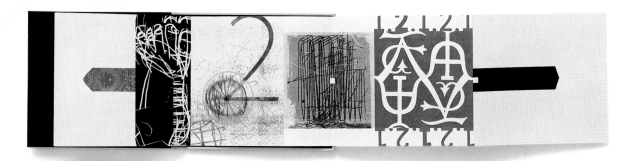

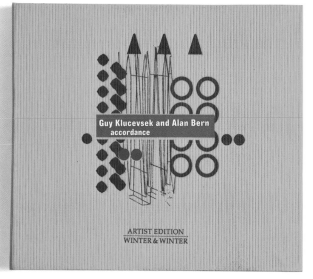

Artist:	Guy Klucevsek and Alan Bern
Label:	Winter & Winter
Design:	Stephen Byram, USA
Effect:	Fine-corrugated, debossed card

Accordance

Designer Stephen Byram regularly designs covers for German label Winter & Winter. Byram created the imagery for this cover digitally, using Photoshop and Illustrator, in about five days. "The music struck me as both contemporary and traditional at the same time, so I tried to do this with the artwork as well," explains Byram. "The cover is me playing with accordion elements in abstract that I hoped felt a bit like the music. I wanted the layout to be very much 'as it happened'." The end result is pretty much that, although a few adjustments to the color and spacing were made before printing to give the cover more rhythm.

Artist: Acoustic Dub Messengers
Label: RAFT MUSIC
Design: FJD (Fujita Jiro Design),
              Japan
Illustration: Yasuko Saito (Acoustic Dub
              Messengers) and FJD
Effect: Blind-embossed and
              embossed card

Mugiminipichi

When commissioned to design this album cover, Japanese designer Jiro Fujita received a felt-pen line drawing of violinist Yasuko Saito. He used this on the cover and as the main inspiration behind the design of the rest of the package.
Fujita created an original typeface for Mugiminipichi's album, also inspired by the organic lines of the drawing, and used an uncoated digipak with black embossed imagery on the front cover, and blind-embossed imagery on the back. "I've heard it costs double to use the digipak in comparison to regular packaging," comments Fujita, "but the owner of RAFT MUSIC, Taro Sasaoka, is a person who cares about packaging as much as sound, so he agreed willingly."

Artist:	King Louis
Label:	Nude Records
Design:	Nitesh Mody and Joe Nixon for Moot, UK
Effect:	Die-cut book format

The Generation I Want

This cover for the King Louis album, The Generation I Want, shows that a carefully considered and interesting design concept can produce a classic, desirable cover while remaining within the confines of the clear jewel case. "The idea was to imply the perfect mould of life," explains cover art director Nitesh Mody. "A lot of the album's lyrics seem to take an honest yet cynical look at society in general and look forward to or hope for something better—The Generation I Want."

Moulds of the two band members' heads enabled wax casts to be made. "The wax material used was a metaphor for the falseness of this life we are embroiled in," explains Mody. After the distinguishing facial features on the moulds had been melted away, they were photographed for use in the booklet both as they were, and also with pictures of the band members' faces projected on to them.

The cover image is a photograph of one of the moulded heads lit from the inside. The die-cut hole on the cover has been placed in the area of the head that the designers interpret the mind to be. The idea is that the hole signifies a missing section from our existing generation— referring to the album title—with the music acting to fill this hole. When the booklet is open and viewed, the holes cast light onto the interior imagery.

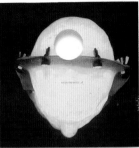

Artists: **Llips** (top left)
Skipsapiens (top right)
Esa Ruoho (bottom left)
Electric Birds (bottom right)
Label: **U-Cover**
Design: **Salt for bombthedot,**
Germany
Illustration: **Salt for bombthedot**
Photography: **Salt for bombthedot**
Effect: **Die-cut series**

Dos Partes (top left)
Untitled (top right)
Spaces (bottom left)
Strata Frames (bottom right)
This series of albums by various
electronic artists was released by Belgian
label U Cover. The aim here was to debut
well-known alternative electronic artists
to provide a showcase of promising talent.
Each cover consists of a four-color
printed, inner card sleeve featuring a
different illustration or photography—
trees, grass, streets and so on—and a
plain outer card sleeve that has the U
Cover logo die-cut into it to reveal the
imagery inside. Arial, Square721, Univers
Condensed, Futura, and Carbon Block
typefaces have been used throughout.

Artist:	Cube Juice
Label:	Happy House
	(Victor Entertainment Inc.)
Design:	Ishiura Masaru for
	TGB Design, Japan
Illustration:	Ishiura Masaru for
	TGB Design
Effect:	Embossed, uncoated card

Called Game (left)
Anything's Gonna Change My World (right)

TGB Design created these covers for the promo single releases by Cube Juice, a fusion of electric, rock and dance music. Ishiura Masaru created city and country landscape imagery for the covers which were then embossed onto the uncoated card stock sleeves. The commercial releases were housed in jewel cases, or P-cases as they are called in Japan, featuring the same illustration except on UV-coated silver paper inserts. TGB also directed the promo video for the release of two of these singles using the same imagery as seen on these covers.

Artist:	Stephan Mathieu and Ekkehard Ehlers
Label:	Brombron / Staalplaat
Design:	Alorenz with Stephan Mathieu, Germany
Effect:	Paper-only packaging

Heroin

The prototype for this folded, paper-only packaging was designed by Dutch company Extrapool. It is an album from the Brombron series, a joint project by Extrapool and German record label Staalplaat, which sees all releases packaged in this way.

Graphic designer Angela Lorenz worked closely with artist Stefan Mathieu to design the cover's graphics. The blue, cream and red pattern is the result of re-mapping colors to the MacOS system colour palette. "A very fascinating process," explains Lorenz. "I never found out exactly how it works but I've been collecting these patterns for a while. I had compiled them for a series so we'll see if I ever get the chance to use them."

> "The size difference between LP and CD design is not a problem; a stamp can be as beautiful and eye-catching as a billboard"

Chris Thomson, Yacht Associates

London-based Yacht Associates was founded in 1996 by Chris Thomson and Richard Bull. It has built up an innovative reputation within the realm of music design, often using strong photography and experimental graphics. It has created a number of award-winning album covers for a range of artists including TLM, Divine Comedy, and Metamatics.

What is your approach to designing an album cover?
We hear the music, talk to the artist and compile a book together of thoughts, directions, doodles, feelings, and solutions —then enthuse about the contents and form an idea. When we design we think of the whole campaign and once you have thought hard about the bigger picture it makes the elements flow and tell a story. The secret is to have a good strong idea and then the medium that it is applied to doesn't matter.

As a designer, how much of a marketing role do you think you play?
The designer's role is to make something attractive, to give it a unique appeal, to capture the essence of the music within, and answer certain marketing boundaries. A poor piece of design occurs when one or more of these properties fails or smothers the others.

How important do you think an album cover is?
I think that if the design is done well then it is integral to the whole attitude; what's cool, what's not, what you want to be associated with and so on. All designers should try and push everything as much as they can. When you are asked to design a CD cover it is your responsibility and opportunity to do so.

With this in mind do you think the CD cover can be made as desirable, or collectable, as vinyl covers?
Special print processes and packaging will make a CD more covetable and designers must always think about what they would like to take home. Small labels allow designers to care more about the covetable longevity of a package, and are aware that a real music lover will treasure something if it is special. It's all about cult appeal. The size difference is not a problem; a stamp can be as beautiful and eye-catching as a billboard. It's about the projection of the concept.

What do you most enjoy about designing an album cover?
The love of telling a story and being part of a sensory experience.

London, 2002

Materials

"Do you like to drink a good wine or whisky out of a plastic cup?"

Stefan Winter, Winter & Winter

Artist: Parva
Label: Mantra Recordings
Design: Alison Fielding for
Beggars Group, UK
Photography: John Zimmerman (top)
Alex Webb, Magnum (centre)
Victoria Collier (bottom)
Effect: Four-color imagery on
reverse-uncoated card

Heavy (top)
Hessles (centre)
Good Bad Right Wrong (bottom)
Parva released these three singles as a
prelude to the album. They were
designed in-house by Alison Fielding, art
director at Beggars Group; she avoided
the jewel case option by using a 300gsm
reverse-uncoated card digipak. Using
reverse card allowed for the four-color
imagery to be applied to the cover without
becoming too glossy, as this was not
suitable for the band. Instead the colors
remain muted, giving the covers a notion
of 70s retro imagery and a more tactile
feel. Fielding wanted to use the initial
image for Heavy as she felt it had a
quality to it that was wonderfully relevant
to the band. To ensure that the same
quality was maintained on each
subsequent release, and that the series
would work as a whole, she sourced all
the images up front. "We didn't want an
obvious interpretation of each single so
each is suggestive rather than being
literal," she explains.

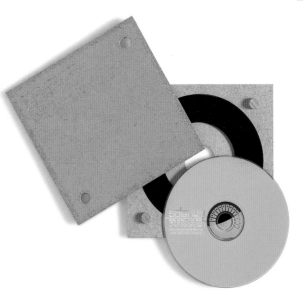

Artist: Solarium
Label: Spezialmaterial
Design: Silvio Waser at Buffer für
Gestaltung (Switzerland)
Effect: MDF and rubber mat

Part 1–14
Sybille Eigenmann encased the ambient
beats of Solarium in this wooden box
because, she says, "Normal CD packaging
is boring." Many of Spezialmaterial's
releases (see also p57) come in innovative
packaging with strong graphics. The
graphic elements were screen-printed
in one color onto the box (made from
relatively inexpensive MDF), while inside,
the disc sits on a rubber mat to prevent
it being damaged by the wood.

Artist: Heads Inc.
Label: Heads Inc.
Design: So Takahashi, USA
Illustration: So Takahashi
Effect: Transparent printed acetate

Heads Inc.

The progressive minimal beats on this CD were made using the basic four-track recording method. To reflect this Takahashi used four transparent layers —front cover, back cover, CD, and CD tray —to make the package. Hundreds of numbers printed in rows on the back cover, and four square shapes that sit together to form a pattern on the front cover, further emphasize the idea of the repetitive beats and four-track recording on the CD inside. Helvetica Bold has been used for the minimal text on the spine.

Artist: Salt
Label: Ant-Zen
Design: Salt for bombthedot, Germany
Photography: Salt for bombthedot
Effect: Foil-embossed, rough-textured card

Re.Wasp

This box was specially designed and produced for this project by German designers Salt. It is made from rough-textured 900gsm black cardboard with silver foil-embossed text on the cover. Once the O card is removed and the inner box is open, a 3-inch CD and series of postcards are revealed. The imagery on the cards show details of organic objects in daily life, and as designer Stefan Alt explained, the idea is to pick up on the small details around us that we are sometimes too busy to notice. The music on this album is experimental electronic, and this edition of it was sold worldwide via specialized experimental electronic music distributors.

Artist:	Bernhard Günter
Label:	LINE
Design:	Richard Chartier, USA
Effect:	Clear plastic sleeve and vellum booklet

Monochrome Rust Differential [right]
**Monochrome White Polychrome
w / neon nails** [bottom]

The packaging design shown here was used for a combination of aesthetic and practical reasons. It consists of a clear plastic sleeve containing a sheet of vellum (Gil Clear) and uncoated card (Cougar Opaque).

Designer Richard Chartier prefers to use slight packaging like this because it suits LINE's releases as the music focuses on minimal sound: "The packaging seems light, is thin and non-obtrusive," explains Chartier, "There are no illusions to it. Also it's a solution to increasing postal costs, and the fact that jewel cases have a greater tendency to break en route to foreign customers. It also allowed us greater flexibility for budget as well."

The titles of the tracks on the four CDs (each release is a double CD) were used as the inspiration for the blocks of color on the front and back of the card. "After discussions with the composer we both agreed that the works themselves were much like paintings, so we gave each of the four sound compositions its own "painting" on their respective packages," reveals Chartier.

The semi-opaque vellum overlay was used on each so that the text would float on top of the 'paintings' and not disturb the fields of color, and, as Chartier says, the sound itself has a very transparent quality.

Artist:	Celluloid Mata
Label:	Ant-Zen
Design:	Salt for bombthedot, Germany
Photography:	Salt for bombthedot
Effect:	Tracing paper cover

Sable

A series of six images of huge rocks sitting on the edge of the St. Malo coast form the imagery within this package. Each is on a separate card made to look like a Polaroid photograph with a white border on the front and a black square on the back. The cards are contained within a tracing paper cover carrying the band's logo, the Mata man, on it. All printing is offset and the typeface is Trebuchet.

Artist:	Various
Label:	Antinos Records
Design:	Groovisions, Japan
Effect:	Solid color jewel cases

Nukes ALTERNATIVE (left)
Nukes GROOVE (right)

"Nukes" is the name of the Korean pop music scene rather than a particular band. Groovisions wanted the cover of these two albums to show a fresh image of Korean pop music. The Nukes logo was printed directly onto solid color jewel cases, and Helvetica Neue typeface was used throughout.

Artist:	Pearl Jam
Label:	Sony
Design:	Brad Klausen, USA

Japan 2003, Seattle Washington November 6 2000, Australia 2003
(from left to right)

In 2000, Pearl Jam released official bootlegs of its live shows. The band's designer, Brad Klausen, designed the CD packaging to look rough and handmade, with no imagery other than lettering on recycled, uncoated card. They play a different set each night, making the bootlegs highly collectable for fans. Says Klausen: "They were pretty much handmade; I hand-stamped all the lettering on the packages using old letterpress letters I found in an antique shop. They all differed in font style and size so no letter was ever the same. If they played Daughter 54 times on the tour, I hand-stamped Daughter 54 times." For the 2003 tour, covers are based on country flags. Again the band wanted them to look like bootlegs. "Their music stands on its own, no elaborate stage design, props or over-the-top lighting," explains Klausen. "Packaging for the bootlegs was designed with that in mind."

Artist:	Gintare
Label:	Parlophone Records
Design:	Jeremy Plumb and Dan Poyner for Traffic, UK
Illustration:	Zena Holloway
Photography:	Zena Holloway
Effect:	Wood and steel

Earthless

As with most special packaging, the budget here was quite generous, allowing Traffic to create a substantial and lavish package for this promo release. Jeremy Plumb worked with Berry Place Models to develop the wood and steel CD case. Imagery in the booklet consists of underwater photographs of Gintare that continue the water idea of the 3-inch samplers (p103). Helvetica Neue typeface was silk-screen printed onto the cover.

Lucky Kitchen

Spanish label Lucky Kitchen is known for its specially packaged releases, the majority of which are limited to a print run of 1000. They avoid the jewel case and use special papers instead, often combined with illustration. The results are delicate, considered packages with a notion of quality to them.

Artist:	Stephan Mathieu
Label:	Lucky Kitchen (lk019)
Design:	Alejandra and Aeron, and Stephan Mathieu, Spain
Illustration:	Stephan and Eva-Lucy Mathieu, and Miriam Rech
Effect:	Textured stock

Die Entdeckung des Wetters

A thick (280gsm) wedding invitation-style paper stock was used for this electro-acoustic pop release. It is a simple design: two folds with the CD tucked away in paper, held in place by a self-adhesive foam holder, and housed in a resealable plastic bag—a packaging option popular in Japan. The minimalist design is an uncomplicated aesthetic preferred by Lucky Kitchen. This package was not overly expensive to produce but became so because of the time it took to assemble.

Artists:	Tetsu Inoue, Stephen Vitiello, and Andrew Deutsch
Label:	Lucky Kitchen (lk017)
Design:	Alejandra and Aeron, Spain
Illustration:	Alejandra and Aeron
Effect:	Plastic vellum information sheet and CD pocket within textured stock

Humming Bird Feeder

This CD package consists of two folds, with the CD placed in the centre, held in place by a triangular plastic "corner". It is made with Verjurado—more commonly used for labelling wine in La Rioja where Lucky Kitchen is based. Track listings have been printed on transparent vellum stock. Swing typeface was used to complement the delicate hand-drawn line illustrations created by the designers.

Artist:	Alejandra and Aeron
Label:	Lucky Kitchen (lk009)
Design:	Alejandra and Aeron, Spain
Illustration:	Alejandra and Aeron
Effect:	Cloth-feel stock, ribbon and sticker

La Rioja

This CD contains recordings of traditional Riojan folk music played in its natural environment: on the streets, in bars, at fiestas, and so on. Designers created an envelope-style package in which to house the CD with the idea of posting it across the globe. A simple red wine-colored sticker holds it closed and a 300gsm stock called Tela (cloth in Spanish) was used. "In this case we wanted a domestic feel to the package that went with the intimacy of the recordings," explains Alejandra. "The piece of ribbon we used came from a very old local lace shop. The proprietor dragged up a roll from the basement, blew the dust off it, and said he was sure we would like it."

Artist:	The Ark
Label:	Virgin Records
Design:	Ricky Tillblad for Zion Graphics, Sweden
Effect:	Colored plastic sheets and flexible, clear-plastic slip case

Calleth You, Cometh I

The intention of this promo release, for Swedish glam rock act The Ark, was to create several different visual effects using transparent materials, strong colors, and strict typography as a base. Designer Ricky Tillblad has used three separate plastic sheets to form a cover held, along with the CD, in a simple slip case. As the cover is unfolded, different visual impressions are created, partly through each separate sheet, but also by moving and combining the sheets in different ways, or looking at them under different lights. The band name and track title was screen-printed in Helvetica Neue 85 onto the sheets.

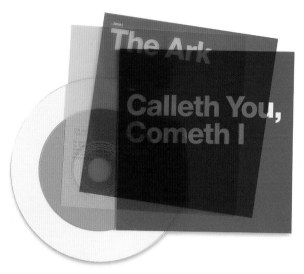

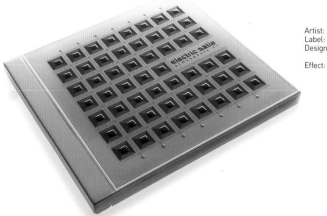

Artist:	Erik Satie
Label:	Victor Entertainment Inc.
Design:	Ishiura Masaru for TGB Design, Japan
Effect:	Printed and embossed solid white jewel case

Electric Satie

This album features techno remixes of Erik Satie's songs. TGB Design created this packaging for the album. In an attempt to express the pure sound of the music, a symmetrical square pattern has been printed and embossed directly onto a solid white jewel case to give it a minimalist, clinical feel with great impact and tactile value. This version of the cover was printed for the first run of CDs and has since sold out. Due to budgetary constraints it has not been produced again.

Artists: Various
Label: Ant-Zen
Design: Salt for bombthedot, Germany
Photography: Salt for bombthedot
Effect: Solid steel with zinc surface

Ant-hology

To celebrate the fifth anniversary of German label Ant-Zen, this compilation of previously unreleased tracks and long out-of-print classics was released. This is the first edition of the compilation and was sold as a limited edition, but it is still available as a regular two-CD set in a jewel case. The metal box was laser-cut and bent to the required dimensions; two regular digipak CD trays hold the CDs. Imagery inside the booklet is from various 1993–1998 Ant-Zen single releases and was applied with copper ink.

Artist: The Vines
Label: Capitol Records
Design: Jan Wilker and Hjalti Karlsson for Karlssonwilker Inc., USA
Illustration: Jan Wilker and Hjalti Karlsson for Karlssonwilker Inc.
Effect: Image-printed shrink-wrap

Highly Evolved

Australian band The Vines has had top ten hits in Europe, the USA, and Australia and this is the packaging for the USA release of Highly Evolved. It consists of a regular shrink-wrapped jewel case featuring unusual imagery. The graphics were silk-screen printed onto the black plastic before application. It took a number of trials to work out the right size to use when applying imagery to the plastic as the designers had to allow for alteration when shrinking. The resulting package is quite different and rather mysterious looking.

Artist:	Joseph Arthur
Label:	Undercover / Virgin Records
Design:	Zachary James Larner for Bombshelter Design, USA
Illustration:	Joseph Arthur
Effect:	Metallic ink on uncoated card

Vacancy

The music of Joseph Arthur is best described as alternative rock. This album cover—a six-panel digipak developed exclusively for this project by designer Zachary James Larner and BigBlue, Portland—features his drawings and paintings. The images were applied to an uncoated charcoal stock using dry-trap, offset printing with a white base, metallic silver, metallic copper, and black. The typography is set in foil letterpress using Badhouse typeface. This limited edition CD received a Grammy nomination in 2000 for Best Package Design.

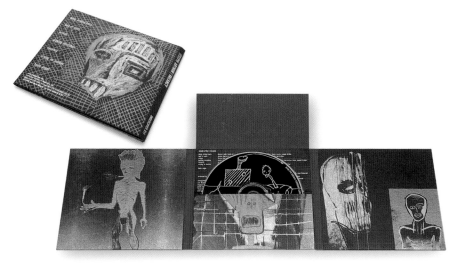

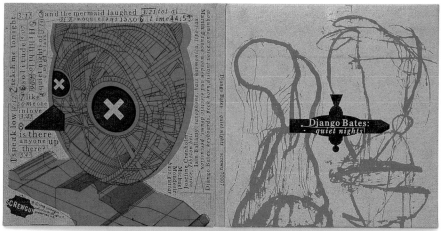

Artist:	Django Bates
Label:	Screwgun
Design:	Stephen Byram
Illustration:	Betsey Berne
Effect:	Letterpress on uncoated card

Quiet Nights

Stephen Byram's work for Screwgun is distinctive not only for the illustration but also for its typographic layouts and use of uncoated board. His intent with these covers is to make personal, interesting, inexpensive, eccentric, and spontaneous packages in an attempt to reflect the spirit of the music and artists that made it. This cover is no exception, made from uncoated card it has a light coat of white on the front cover and has been printed using letterpress.

Artists: **Tim Berne, Tom Rainey,
and Drew Gress**
Label: **Screwgun**
Design: **Stephen Byram, USA**
Illustration: **Stephen Byram**
Effect: **Uncoated stock**

Please Advise

The illustration for this CD cover is by
Stephen Byram. It relates to the album's
title, Please Advise, and to the
relationship troubles Byram was
experiencing. "I guess it's about things
looking one way and being another, and
the confining structures we hide in,"
explains Byram. He used Trade Gothic
and AG Old typefaces, and ran the band
members' names upside-down on the
cover to help separate them from the
band name and title.

Artist: **Bazeado**
Label: **Mr Bongo**
Design: **Red Design, UK**
Effect: **Uncoated, embossed board**

Requebra Nega

Red Design used an uncoated card
booklet and slip case as packaging for
Bazeado's album and single. Bazeado
is the music of Pedro Martins, a Brazilian
living in the UK, writing and producing
Brazilian music. Designers at Red
chose Meadcote card and simple solid
color prints to convey the earthy
Latin-American nature of the music.
The typeface, developed by Red, was
embossed on the sleeve together with
imagery of Martins' son playing with
instruments used on the album.

Artists:	Various
Label:	4 Foot 11 / Extasy Records International
Design:	TJ River and Todd Gallopo for Meat and Potatoes, USA
Effect:	Uncoated brown craft stock and rubberstamp lettering

Sampler / Advance

Design company Meat and Potatoes used the uncoated brown craft paper stock that printers normally employ to wrap finished jobs, as covers for this series of DJ remix compilation samplers. The aim of the series was to introduce the music to radio stations before the albums appeared in-store, so it was important to make the design distinctive. Meat and Potatoes chose to take this paper bag-like approach to the design, as it has a significantly different feel to the high-gloss packages typical of this genre. Bookman, Ariston, and Snell typefaces were all applied by hand, using specially made rubberstamps.

Artist:	Tim Berne
Label:	Screwgun
Design:	Stephen Byram, USA
Illustration:	Stephen Byram
Effect:	Metallic ink and uncoated card

Empire Box

This five disc reissue of Tim Berne's music from 1979 to 1982 is, according to Byram, a monumentally historic record of his growing-up. The design is a spoof of seals, formal marks, icons, and symbols. Byram took Berne's original logo for Empire Records and eroded it, allowing it to develop into a new form incrementally over the five discs. Screwgun's printer and collaborator John Upchurch designed the actual folding configuration of the package and suggested using metallic copper ink to apply text and imagery.

Artist: A Certain Frank
Label: ata tak / EFA 03771
Design: Frank Fenstermacher,
Germany
Illustration: Frank Fenstermacher
Effect: Q-Tip contained in
color-printed, solid white
jewel case

Nobody? No! (top)
Nothing (bottom)

The music on both albums shown here by A Certain Frank is described as a mixture of pop, lounge, and jazz. The first album, Nobody? No!, was released in 1999, a time when Fenstermacher felt that the majority of CD packages in-store were either colorful or dark. To ensure the CD would stand out he designed a lighter, largely white package. "The idea was to work in a subtle way to show a kind of innocence; that is why I chose to use the two pictograms to symbolize the musicians," he says. A Q-Tip is included in the spine of the tray as it works with the package's colors and it relates to the ears with which you hear the music.

The second album, entitled Nothing, was released in 2001 with a far more colorful cover. "Times, colors, and tastes change," comments Fenstermacher, "and also this time I felt that the music was more colorful. I loved orange then so I combined it with blue. It wasn't so easy to find the third colour, pink, but we did." The idea is based on being able to see all three dimensions of the CD at one time—the cover, disc, and tray. Continuing this theme Fenstermacher has again used three pictogram heads within the package; two at the front that face each other when the case is opened, and a typographic arrangement of the track listings makes up another on the back.

Artist:	Solotempo (left)
	6000 / SM (right)
Label:	Spezialmaterial
Design:	Chiara Nikish and Tobias
	Peier, Switzerland
Effect:	Hand-sewn, transparent
	plastic (left)
	Hand-sewn, modified
	potato chip packet (right)

Oct:Ten (left)
Eins (right)

Spezialmaterial are known for their unique handmade CD covers (see also p45). Oct:Ten, shown here, consists of a card sleeve and an outer transparent plastic cover with hand-sewn edges. The cover for Eins was made from a potato chip packet and again has hand-stitched edges. Spezialmaterial takes great pride in its covers and its music. In an interview with online magazine Loop, Cio Assereto of Spezialmaterial explains why: "It is the interest we have for packaging, working with new materials, new designs we'd like to create, and different kinds of covers, but it's a matter of time and money. We don't have a pressure for every cover to be special. It happens if the idea is new and we feel like doing it."

Artists:	Various
Label:	Ministry of Sound
Design:	Amp Associates, UK
Illustration:	Amp Associates
Effect:	Debossing and
	gold foil-blocking

The Karma Collection

This is a double CD compilation of chill-out dance music with an eastern influence released by the Ministry of Sound. It is aimed specifically at a spiritual / healthy-living female market aged 25+. The flock wallpaper in Indian restaurants and the Hindu God Krishna inspired Amp Associates in its design of the package. A fabric-coated stock and gold foil-embossed Davida type is used on the cover, produced by London Fancy Box, to give the package an element of luxury and strong in-store impact.

Artist:	Green Day
Label:	Warner Bros.
Design:	Chris Bilheimer, USA
Illustration:	Chris Bilheimer, Marina Chavez
Photography:	Chris Bilheimer, Marina Chavez

Warning

Chris Bilheimer used the plastic bags that his Macintosh monitor software came in as inspiration for this Green Day cover. The plastic green cover with screen-printed images opens to reveal a 40-page book and CD housed in a cardboard folder.

Artists:	Various
Label:	12k
Design:	Taylor Deupree for 12k, USA
Package Design:	Dan Abrams
Effect:	Mylar laser-cut pack with plastic sheet insert

.aiff

Made from Mylar, this package is cut like an old 5¼-inch floppy disc, (which is also 12k's logo), so it can be opened on three of its four sides. "The idea was to use the label logo as the package design itself," says Taylor Deupree. "The transparency reflects the music quite well; minimalism is the nature of the music, and the label's aesthetic. The packaging is very important and must tie in well." A clear plastic sheet inside contains all the text (in Emigre Eight and Franklin Gothic). Not only did this release sell out very quickly, it also signalled a change in 12k's design and music consciousness. It got the label noticed as a leading contributor to minimalist electronic music and firmly established them as a leader of design-conscious labels in the USA.

Artist: White Trash
Label: Black Agitator
Design: Peter and Paul, UK
Photography: Peter and Paul
Effect: Board, foam, photocopied paper, plastic sheets, and staples

White Trash

White Trash is described by Peter and Paul as savage, primitive, neo-futurist, electro-attack punk with a very raw, gritty sound. To capture this atmosphere in the packaging, they handmade the covers using a mix of materials they found in their studio. Only 30 were made and distributed to promoters and press. The poster features photographs of the band playing their first live gig in Reykjavik, Iceland, as part of the Desperate Sound System Tour, organized by Jarvis Cocker and Steve Mackey of Pulp.

Artist: **Ram Jam World**
Label: **Warner Music Japan**
Design: **Groovisions, Japan**
Effect: **Uncoated stock** (left)
and postal pack (right)

Uso Tsukina Hadaka (left)
Re. (right)

Ram Jam World is a pop / drum 'n' bass
act backed by Hirofumi Asamoto, a
well-known Japanese musician.
Groovisions designed these two packs
for them, one of which is a padded postal
pack specially designed and made for this
project. Sold commercially in-store, the
idea was simply to do something a
bit different for the release of this album.

Artists: **Various**
Label: **Polyvinyl Records, USA**
Design: **Greg Burnstein for
Hydrafuse, USA**
Effect: **Metallic ink on
uncoated stock**

Re Direction

The use of near colors and clean type on
this cover for Polyvinyl is heavily inspired
by the work of Swiss designer Joseph
Müller-Brockman, particularly his Zurich
Tonhalle posters of the 60s. Helvetica
Neue typeface was used throughout to
replicate the classic Swiss design style
and three color variations of uncoated
stock were chosen for the insert and tray
card. Originally Burnstein wanted to use
a white ink for the type but due to an
error during the print process, a metallic
silver ink was used instead. Luckily it
worked equally well.

"If the music is great, a great package can really make the experience transcendent"

Stephen Byram

Stephen Byram has been designing music packages for over 20 years. He is perhaps best known for his covers for New York label Screwgun Records and German label Winter & Winter, but he also works for Sony USA, creating covers for artists including the Beastie Boys, Indigo Girls, and Slayer.

How do you approach the design of an album cover and what inspires you?
I try to be as open as I can with it, and take inspiration from the music, things I experience, things I find out, and my relationships with the people I work with on projects.

Do you prefer working for independent or mainstream record labels?
Well Screwgun and Winter & Winter (independents) see the package as an opportunity to make some art as well as convey information. At their best they become part of the expression of the music. It's a much simpler process; there aren't many layers of approval or agendas to consider. Also, independents aren't concerned with mass appeal and speak to a sympathetic audience. Major labels are concerned with selling to a mass of people, and think that the package should look like something that many will want to buy. It is also made more complicated by an ocean of opinion that must be addressed and reconciled. Matters of aesthetics and expression are not very high on the list, or as an executive in the record business once said: "Make no mistake, it is about commerce not art."

What do you most enjoy about designing album covers?
I love music, I love creating things and being part of something larger than myself. I've been fortunate to be involved with a group of people who share this purpose.

Can the CD be made as desirable and collectable an item as the old vinyl?
Yes, this has been accomplished many times. Designers should work as honestly and creatively as they can and as the situation permits. If they make something important and this is recognised it will be collectable, if not now, then later. It's not possible to make something collectable by force of will alone.

How important do you think an album cover is? Does it influence sales?
Covers don't sell records, music does. If the music is good, a good package will extend the experience. If the music is great, a great package can really make the experience transcendent. Both situations definitely make people feel they got something for their hard-earned cash, and encourages them to try it again.

What sort of image do you think makes the best cover?
The one that works best. There is no formula.

Any more thoughts or issues you'd like to raise?
Yes, I wish that the music business would stop seeing the fast food industry as a role model.

New York, 2002

Interaction

"Strong creativity will usually find a way of bending rules and finding new ways of expression"

Jon Forss, Non-Format

Artist: **MEEM**
Label: **Non-recordings**
Design: **MEEM, Australia**
Illustration: **MEEM**
Photography: **MEEM**
Effect: **Plywood, felt, Velcro, and stamping**

MEEM

Plywood—stained and unstained—brown felt, Velcro, printed paper, an ink stamp, and a hot stamp were all used to make this CD package by Australian artist and designer, Michael Mobus. The project was extremely time- and labor-intensive, as each pack was handmade. Four wood squares were stained twice before cutting and then glued to the felt and Velcro dot fasteners. The wooden surface of the front cover was burnt with a hot stamp insignia bearing the MEEM logo. Two more rubber stamps containing information were applied before each copy was sanded and hand-numbered.

Artist: **Tin Foil Star**
Label: **Staalplaat**
Design: **Alorenz, Germany**
Effect: **Paper stud binder**

Mort Aux Vaches series

The paper binder is not a practical or possible solution for many releases, but for the Mort Aux Vaches series (see also p36 and p74), released on German label Staalplaat, it has proved to be a simple yet effective solution to holding the folded card packages closed. The binder is fed through a die-cut hole in the front cover, a further die-cut hole in the third flap, the hole in the middle of the CD, and the die-cut hole in the back cover. This particular cover was designed by Angela Lorenz. The text was foil-embossed onto the cover and the imagery used inside was found in a box of abandoned slides at a flea market. This copy is part of a limited-release run of 1000.

Artist: Various
Label: Kriztal Entertainment
Design: Karlssonwilker Inc., USA
Effect: Belly-band and
    barcode-printed CD

Elemental Chill

The design idea behind this series of chill-out compilation albums is the four elements: fire, earth, water, and air, each of which is represented by its own logo and color. The logos were created using the same grid as the pixel typeface used for the album titles. Karlssonwilker used a regular digipak with a matt exterior to house the discs. They also used belly-bands because, as designer Jan Wilker explains, "It makes it more of a package, like a gift box with something in it."

Like many other design companies who have used the belly-band, Karlssonwilker avoided printing text on the front cover of the package, and because of the desire to keep the design minimal, there is little text elsewhere. However, retailers felt that the single barcode on the belly-band might get lost. The retailers requested that an additional working barcode appear somewhere else on the package. In order to retain the minimalist look of the cover and not "spoil" it with a barcode, Karlssonwilker applied them directly onto the discs in a series of circles, as shown here, that do actually work when they are scanned in-store.

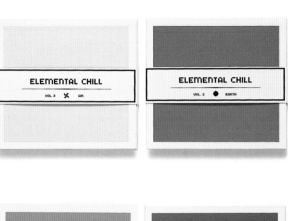

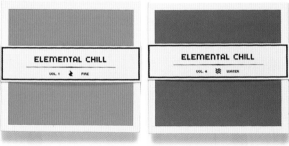

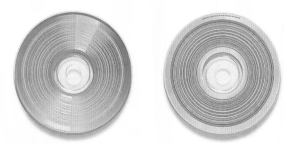

Artist:	Tomas Jirku
Label:	intr_version records
Design:	Aaron McConomy, Canada
Photography:	Mitchell Akiyama and Aaron McConomy
Effect:	Matchbook-style opening and stitching

Entropy

Intr_version calls this the "matchbook" CD cover since its design principle is the same; only these packages are sewn, rather than stapled or glued, as with most actual matchbooks. The label outsourced the printing and cutting but did all the assembling and sewing of the packages in-house. "As a niche label you need a strong packaging concept to set yourself apart from the masses," explains label art director Aaron McConomy. "Jewel cases just don't cut it unless you're a major label pressing 100,000 copies per run. Also in a post-MP3 world the main reason to buy a CD is to own a beautiful object. Unless you put out something special people will just download it." Other advantages are that they are smaller and lighter than jewel cases;

the label's mailing costs have dropped around 80 percent since they started using the matchbook case. It is also around 20 percent cheaper per unit than jewel cases. The releases make use of various different images that relate to the music on each CD. They are sold internationally, mainly in boutique and speciality record stores.

Artist:	Rothko
Label:	Lo Recordings
Design:	EkhornForss / Non-Format, UK
Photography:	Photodisc
Effect:	Sticker to tear

Forty Years to Find a Voice

The idea for this CD package was to keep it as clean and abstract as possible. A sticker, containing all the text on the cover, acts as a seal and also presents the owner with a decision about how to get to the CD inside—should they slit it open at the side or remove the sticker entirely? The imagery shows two different cow furs and bear fur to fulfil the brief of creating a cover that seemed abstract at first glance, but was actually specific on examination. The track listing is repeated on the inside of the package and the hope was that consumers would remove the

sticker once they got it home to leave the packaging covered almost entirely with fur. A simple font (Letter Gothic) was used, and text was cropped off the back to suggest that each sticker had been cut from a much longer roll of stickers. This subtle hint at automation adds a harder edge to the package to contrast with the soft organic fur images.

Artist: **My Computer**
Label: **13 Amp Records**
Design: **Sarah Hopper, UK**
Illustration: **Kate Gibb**
Effect: **Origami game insert**

Vulnerabilia

This eclectic imagery is a series of screenprints by Kate Gibb who has also worked on covers for The Chemical Brothers and Simian. The images reflect the music on the CD and are printed in CMYK plus a fifth fluorescent color. Hopper was keen for the consumer to interact with the package so included a simple childhood paper game.

Artist: **The Strokes**
Label: **RCA Records**
Design: **Brett Kilroe and Robin Hendrickson at RCA Records, USA**

Someday

The cover image for the Someday single taken from the album Is This It, is from a stained glass window designed by architect Frank Lloyd Wright. Perhaps the band's decision to use preexisting images from the worlds of fine art, architecture, and design, can be seen as an attempt to place its music within the context of high culture.

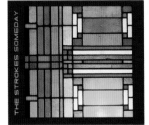

Artist: **The Strokes**
Label: **RCA Records**
Design: **The Strokes**

Last Nite

This cover incorporates a detail from a painting by James Rosenquist, a 60s Pop Art painter. His work anticipates digital image manipulation decades prior to its invention causing an imbalance between the retro qualities of such imagery and its apparent modernity. This is echoed in The Strokes' music that is colored with shades of earlier bands but is undeniably fresh and distinct.

Artist:	Block
Label:	Capitol Records
Design:	Stefan Sagmeister and Hjalti Karlsson, USA
Photography:	Susan Stava, Barbara Ehrbar, and Gudmundur Ingolfsson
Effect:	A cigarette trapped in the spine

Timing is Everything

Sagmeister's trademark handwriting appears in the booklet of this album for electronic pop band Block. There is a cigarette in the spine and a clock in the centre of each CD. The clock can be set to different times simply by moving the CD around in its holder. The inclusion of a cigarette was inspired by Jamie Block after spending an afternoon discussing the music with Stefan Sagmeister; Block returned to tell Sagmeister that he forgot to mention he really likes to smoke Rothmans' (cigarettes). Sagmeister felt that imagery wasn't enough and that the real thing should be included. This nearly didn't happen at production stage when workers refused to put the cigarettes in the spines of the case fearing the nicotine would enter their bloodstreams through their skin. Capitol Records had to supply them with surgical gloves before they would go ahead and pack them.

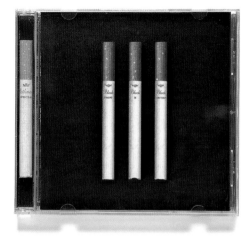

Artist: Bovine Life + / vs. Komet
Label: Fällt + / vs. Bip-Hop
Design: Fehler, Ireland
Illustration: Fehler
Effect: Innovative print-positioning to give equal billing

Bovine Life + / vs. Komet

Chris Murphy, Fällt founder and designer at Fehler, co-curates this series of split CDs with Philippe Petit of Bip-Hop. The packaging design needed to reflect the fact that the series is about collaboration, and that the artists on each release are equally respected. One of the challenges was to find a way in which to print both artists' names twice on the packaging, in two different orders: Komet + / vs. Bovine Life and Bovine Life + / vs. Komet. Starting with the type, Petit and Murphy then looked at how the same idea could be applied to the packaging itself—hence the two covers, two spines, and two ways that information on the disc can be viewed. "Once I began to experiment with laying out the type in two different orders

it was a natural progression to think of the packaging itself as being reversible: two front covers, two back covers, and so on," explains Murphy. "I originally hoped to create a custom die-cut package to further underline the reversible artwork concept, but unfortunately this proved too expensive. In the end we used a digipak. For this particular reversible concept a jewel case would not have worked as it cannot be opened either way up."

The concept carries through to the cover graphic and typographic layout. The intention was to create a pattern for the series that was instantly recognizable and easily applied in two colors—one for each artist. Again, the typography is

intended to enhance the booklet's physicality. The Komet and the Bovine Life information is orientated in opposite ways. Production costs for this package were greater than if using a jewel case but Murphy believes that aesthetics should not be compromised by cost. "My attitude to packaging, especially for CDs, is to ensure that the right packaging for the specific piece is used, regardless of cost, where possible."

Artist: **Placebo**
Label: **Hut Recordings**
Design: **Hut Recordings, UK**
Photography: **Kevin Westenberg**
Pack design: **Burgopak**
Effect: **Innovative print-positioning to give equal billing**

Black Market Music

This is a limited-edition album release by Placebo entitled Black Market Music. The graphic elements of the cover were designed in-house at the band's label Hut Recordings, but the innovative packaging was designed by Burgopak and produced by Artomatic. The package has a patented opening mechanism—by pulling on a tab the package opens at opposite ends of the cover with the disc tray to the left and booklet tray to the right. It works by way of a belt-drive mechanism inside the case, and, by pushing the same tab, the disc tray and booklet tray are simultaneously returned to the case and the package is closed. When this all-card package was released in 2000 around 85,000 copies of the album were sold in four days.

Artist: **Bulbul**
Label: **Trost**
Design: **Moussi Bucy, Austria**
Effect: **Hinged iron with nut and bolt fastenings**

Bulbul

This heavy, solid, iron cover with bolt fastening was designed by Moussi Bucy for Austrian rock band Bulbul. Colorful imagery on the disc is in stark contrast to the rest of the package which, if dropped, is more likely to damage the floor than itself. The type on the covers of the 1500 copies that were produced was applied with a set of metal stamps. The package is designed to rust over time.

Artist: **Various**
Label: **Hydrogen Dukebox Records**
Design: **Yacht Associates, UK**
Photography: **Yacht Associates**
Effect: **Opaque, colored jewel boxes sealed with stickers**

Buy Me Try Me

The idea behind this was to make a statement about consumerism and waste. Solid color opaque jewel cases were used to create a package that appears luxurious but the day-glo punk colored stickers are photographs of discarded shopping trolleys and garbage. By sealing the jewel case with a sticker the designers intended to make it virginal and precious. "You don't really want to tear it open but you have to," explains Chris Thomson.

Artists:	Various
Label:	Independent release by Alexander McQueen
Design:	Oliver Walker for Walker Gellender and Artomatic, UK
Illustration:	Oliver Walker for Walker Gellender and Artomatic
Photography:	Anne Deniau
Effect:	Screw-fastened acrylic discs

10

Each one of the ten tracks on this limited-edition of 300 CDs was used for one of fashion designer Alexander McQueen's catwalk shows. For the purposes of this album the tracks were remixed by John Gosling. The brief for Oliver Walker was originally to produce an invitation for the launch of the newly opened McQueen shop in New York. However, McQueen also wanted him to develop a product based around the invite that could be given away at the opening.

The clear discs are cut-and-polished, 10mm thick sheet acrylic. There is a male and female disc; the male disc has a thread that screws into the female. The CD was screen-printed in matt black onto the black polycarbon disc. The body of the clear acrylic CD holder was printed with a clear matt vinyl extender base to effect an etched look. "The design of the packaging is purely to create something as extravagant for CD packaging as would be created for a McQueen collection," according to Walker. "This elevates the CD to coffee table display item as opposed to providing another CD to be put in the collection."

Artist:	**Peter Herbert and David Tronzo**
Label:	**Azizamusic**
Design & Digital Image Composition:	**Elisabeth Kopf, Austria with Werner Korn, USA**
Effect:	**Scratch-off imagery**

Segmente

Elisabeth Kopf and Werner Korn designed this cover for Peter Herbert and David Tronzo's album Segmente. The cover was designed to conceal a secret that one can only reveal by permanently damaging the top surface of the cover. Kopf and Korn also wanted to create a cover that could be distinctively personalized by the owners of the CD so they designed a "scratched surface". The scratch-off cover consists of two images printed on top of each other; it consists of eight printed layers altogether including a seal to prevent the hidden image from being scratched off. The inclusion of a coin or "scratch tool" references lottery scratch cards. Only one in ten of the CD packages contains a coin.

The faces of the two men on the cover are those of the musicians (Peter Herbert on the right, David Tronzo on the left). However, the body of the two men is that of designer Korn's, and when scratched the revealed imagery is quite different from expected. "I don't want to totally reveal the secret of the image underneath," explains Kopf. "I'd like to describe it this way: if you take the risk to look behind the surface you will not always find what you expect."

Artist:	Pulseprogramming
Label:	Aesthetics
Design:	John Shachter with Hans Seeger, USA
Illustration:	John Shachter with Hans Seeger
Printing:	Blanchette Press
Effect:	Tyvek® model kit

Tulsa For One Second

The focus here was on exploring structural boundaries. "The music is based on a traditional song-writing style, containing more warmth than Pulse programming's typical electronic sound, making the listen more intimate and hospitable," comments Hans Seeger. "We wanted the packaging to reflect that by manifesting those traits—tradition, warmth, hospitality, and so on; we opted for illustration over photography, for a homemade, modest look and feel."

The package was printed by Blanchette Press, offset (2-color) on Tyvek®. It was then mounted, scored, and folded onto a thin substrate. Helvetica Neue type was used throughout. "It's always encouraging to do something new," adds Seeger. "Such as creating your own format versus retrofitting one idea into another. Also, jewel cases are too wasteful to feel good about utilizing, in my opinion."

Artist:	Green Day
Label:	Warner Bros.
Design:	Chris Bilheimer, USA
Illustration:	Snorri Bros.
Photography:	Snorri Bros.

Redundant

Green Day's Redundant single was taken from the 1997 Nimrod album; this is the promotional version of the CD single. Working on a small budget, Chris Bilheimer's challenge was to create a cheap but interesting cover. "I used the same art on both the transparent sticker and the CD label," he explains. "The sticker creates a low-budget 3D effect when the CD face is properly lined up."

Artist:	Ryoji Ikeda
Label:	Staalplaat
Design:	Alorenz, Germany
Effect:	Plastic nipple fastening

Mort Aux Vaches series

This is another package in Staalplaat's Mort Aux Vaches series designed by Angela Lorenz. Polypropylene was used here instead of card. The folding configuration remains the same as that seen on p36 and p63, except this time the three panels and a CD are held together in the middle by a plastic nipple rather than a paper binder.

The type was laid out as clearly and simply as possible on the cover to complement the interface on the back. This consists of two patterns, circles and spirals, that have been printed on the sleeve and the disc—placed together they create a moiré effect. The imagery and text was screen-printed onto the polypropylene but not without difficulty. It took five attempts to find an ink that would take to the plastic. "The manufacturer of the plastic claimed it was printable, but in reality it wasn't so easy," explains Lorenz. "If you ever want to print on plastic I wouldn't recommend using polypropylene, use PVC instead."

Artist:	David Byrne
Label:	Luaka Bop / Virgin Records
Creative Director:	Stephen Doyle at Doyle Partners, USA
Design:	John Clifford at Doyle Partners
Illustrators:	Jia Hwang and Stephen Doyle

U.B. Jesus

Designers at New York-based design house Doyle Partners turned an image of musician David Byrne into a paint-by-numbers picture for the cover of his U.B. Jesus single, from the Look into the Eyeball album. They manipulated a photograph of the artist in Photoshop and Illustrator to produce a blue line illustration that was then partly filled in. The cover image was left unfinished and included in the CD case was a color key so that whoever bought the CD was able to paint in the remaining colors his or herself.

Artist: Andrei Zueff
Label: Frogman Records
Design: Hideaki Komiyama and Masashi Ichifuru for TGB Design, Japan
Illustration: Hideaki Komiyama and Masashi Ichifuru for TGB Design
Effect: Card-only presentation pack

Kitchen Works

This packaging is a great example of an alternative to the jewel case. It is solid, sturdy and, because of the way the disc is held, also protects it from scratch damage. The case was designed to push up and present the CD to the viewer as it is opened, made possible by a simple folding configuration. It cost less than a jewel case and was released commercially in Japan.

Artist: Various
Label: Rex Records
Design: Airside, UK
Illustration: Airside
Effect: Belly-band

If I Was Prince

Airside was commissioned to design the packaging for this CD of Prince cover versions. It had to allude to Prince without using any actual images of him due to copyright issues. So, the designers created pixelated versions of his most recognizable album sleeves. If viewed from quite a distance the original sleeves begin to become legible. The song titles are in Preset typeface and illustrated by small pixel people to give the sleeve personality. These characters, created in Photoshop and Illustrator, were also used on the website, where they dance around. Using a belly-band enabled Airside to create a largely purple sleeve (a color strongly linked to Prince) with very little type on it, as most of the copy is on the belly-band.

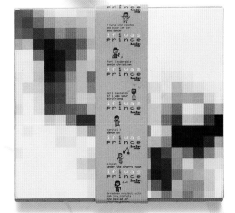

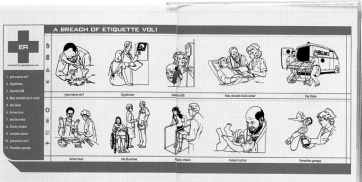

Artist:	Various
Label:	Etiquette Recordings (Outside Inc.)
Design:	Ishiura Masaru for TGB Design, Japan
Illustration:	Ken Hamaguchi
Effect:	O card and instructional illustration

A Breach of Etiquette

Shortened to its initials, record label Etiquette Recordings becomes ER; in English these initials are more commonly associated with Emergency Room, hence the hospital-inspired design of this release. Tokyo-based TGB Design has used Japanese illustrator Ken Hamaguchi's simple airline safety card instructional-style line drawings to illustrate this lounge music compilation. Clean and simple use of color gives the package a functional and instructional look, and the use of an O card allows the cover imagery to be seen clearly, as opposed to through a plastic jewel case.

Artist: **Pinebender**
Label: **Ohio Gold Records**
Design: **Andy Mueller for**
Ohio Girl Design, USA
Effect: **Pencil and paper included**
for a DIY cover

Too Good to Be True

This cover is a great example of how a simple and relatively inexpensive idea can provide the user with more than just a listening experience. This CD package demands interaction: "The main idea of this packaging is to explore the relationship between the product, consumer, and designer," reveals Andy Mueller. "I wanted to see how the consumer would react to a 'Do-It-Yourself' CD cover."

Included with each CD is a small pencil and pad of graph paper; the idea being that the consumer draws his or her own CD cover with the materials provided. Helvetica typeface was used throughout, as Mueller wanted to use a simple, classic font that would create a neutral, instructional tone for the design. The handwriting on the tray card was done by the lead singer of the band on Mueller's request as he thought it would be interesting to personalize part of the packaging.

"The interior design obviously has little effect on the buying decision—I see it as a little gift to the viewer"

Stefan Sagmeister, Sagmeister Inc.

Originally from Austria, Stefan Sagmeister is one of the world's most prolific graphic designers. Since he formed the New York-based Sagmeister Inc. in the early 80s, his music industry design work for, most notably, The Rolling Stones, David Byrne, Pat Metheny, and Lou Reed, has seen him nominated for four Grammies, and he has won a multitude of international design awards.

When approaching the design of an album cover, what inspires you and how do you attempt to translate and represent the music in a piece of artwork?
We talk to the band and in this initial meeting I try to avoid talking about the cover itself, instead focusing on the music, their inspiration for it, the lyrics, and where it came from. We then listen to the music a lot while designing the package.

How much of a role does the designer play as marketer in the retail environment?
It is considered, but most frequently only in silly rules like the band name placed in the top third of the CD—so it is visible when flicking through trays. There are no reliable numbers out there proving the influence of the packaging on sales. This is a real pity because I might (if I'm right that the cover is influential) use those numbers as a handy tool in my fight with marketing executives who generally only listen to numbers.

The potential customer doesn't see the main bulk of artwork as it is inside. How does this affect the design concept, if at all?
We take the inside very seriously and often lavish a lot of love and care on it. Because it is not seen on the outside and so obviously has little effect on the buying decision, I see it as a little gift to the viewer.

What is it that you most enjoy about designing a CD package?
The small format; as a designer you can put a lot of love into something very portable. And the large numbers of printed copies; I can find it here, in Bombay, in Reykjavik, wherever. The fact that it does not get thrown out; this is very rare in the world of graphic design. And, you can come up with a concept just by listening to music.

Can the CD pack ever be as desirable, or as collectable as vinyl?
I have about 500 CDs and used to have roughly the same amount of albums. If I pulled out some of the great designs from each category I'd wind up with about the same amount of good pieces. The CD will be as dead as the vinyl album in about five years from now. However, fans will still collect it.

Music largely remains packaged in jewel cases. What can be done to make them more distinctive or innovative?
It's all just a matter of money. I have a small collection of special packaging with covers made out of metal, wood, concrete, and so on. I never found this category that interesting, it is easy to do unusual work if you can use any unusual material so therefore most concepts rely too much on production issues.

What type of image do you think makes a good cover?
The one that touches the viewer. This can be done with type only: XTC GO 2 by Hipgnosis; with illustration—King Crimson, In the Court of the Crimson King; or with photography—The Rolling Stones, or Sticky Fingers by Andy Warhol.

New York, 2002

"With the introduction of a new artist the sleeve design is extremely important"

The Client: Terry Felgate, Parlophone Records

Terry Felgate is Director of Marketing and Creative for Parlophone. He has been working in the industry for over 15 years with artists including Blur, Coldplay, Kylie, Radiohead, The Pet Shop Boys, and Beverley Knight.

How important do you think the album cover is?
I believe that the images associated with music are part of the complete picture. So many albums are remembered for their sleeves as well as their music, but however good a sleeve, it's unlikely to be remembered unless the album achieves a certain level of success.

With the introduction of a new artist the sleeve design is extremely important. If a person is being asked to take a chance on a new album where they have maybe only heard one track or read some press reviews, then the artwork plays a crucial role in giving a wider impression of what they can expect to hear. I have read reviews before which have caught my interest. If the sleeve fits with the impression I have of the album then that can be the final persuading point for me.

How do you approach the briefing of designers?
We will often pitch a project out to two or three design teams with a brief and then review pitches and present them to the artist. Once we have agreed on a designer, we will meet with them and the artist and discuss ideas. The designer will then present ideas for the single and / or album and we will feed back comments from the artist, and from ourselves. However, we do try and find designers that we are confident in, so we feel able to give them space to develop their ideas.

Are decisions about covers based on their marketability or the design aesthetic?
The marketability does need to be considered: Is it a strong image? Can you read the artist's name and title? But the design takes prominence. It also really varies from artist to artist and genre to genre. For "pop" artists like Kylie for instance, you tend to want to feature them on the sleeve. Whereas for rock bands or dance artists this is less important. A strong concept can be more effective here, for example on Coldplay's covers.

The drop in record sales over the past few years has been attributed to the availability of downloadable music. What do you see as the solution to this potential problem?
I think the way people consume music will continue to change. People will continue to buy CDs but they will also become more used to consuming music digitally. Record companies will need to begin to make music much more available in digital format through paid-for systems of distribution.

Do you have a preferred CD packaging format?
The jewel case is extremely practical. I don't think it should be replaced but it's good to see new forms of packaging too.

London, 2002

03

"CDs work on two levels, a distinctive hit in the store, then an unravelling of the story"

Richard Hales, Michael Nash Associates

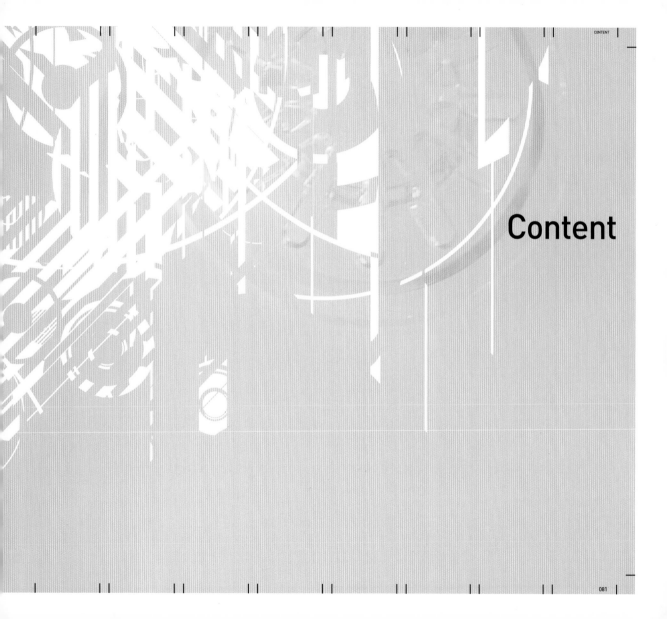

Content

"I always keep in mind what musicians want to express above all. I am inspired by sound. The most important thing is mutual understanding"

Hideaki Komiyama, TGB Design

Introduction

The nature of the CD package means that the consumer is unable to see the bulk of the artwork until it is unwrapped. The cover should be intriguing, seducing the potential customer with the possibility of what is inside. Once the shrinkwrap is removed, the interior should give adequate reward both in terms of the music, and text and imagery. It is important, particularly with the advent of downloadable music, that consumers get something from the artwork that gives the album extra meaning, something that cannot be gleaned from an MP3.

It is with this in mind that the artwork on the following pages was selected. These examples add something to the buying experience. This extra pleasure in imagery and text reveals more about the artist than the words of the songs alone. Few of the covers feature straightforward band photographs, but are instead graced with images created by a very diverse range of people. These include Laurent Fetis (p92) and Fred Deakin (p91), experimental and abstract photographers like Dominic Davies for 4AD (p93) and Wolfgang Tillmans (p110), and artists such as Yoshitomo Nara (p86). Album cover design has also provided a platform for many fine artists in the past, for example Julian Opie (for Blur) and Julian Shnabel (for Red Hot Chili Peppers). The combination of fine art and cutting-edge music often results in memorable and iconic imagery, raising the profile of both musician and artist.

Of course the designer also produces imagery, but his or her primary concern after layout is typography. Type on CDs performs two roles: it entertains and it informs. While designers have the freedom to commission or produce the imagery, the text is often dictated by the band or the record label, and must be included as supplied. Track listings, lyrics, band histories, credits, prayers, stories... the list is endless, and the designer's

task is to work this mass of information into an interesting, usable form within the constraints of the medium—the pack, with its front and back, and possibly an enclosed booklet. There are always exceptions to the normal management of CD pack copy, in some instances the designer decides what and how much text should be included. This was the case with UK designers Milk, when creating the cover for compilation album Futurism. Here, designers and writers developed a dictionary definition of the term "Futurism" and used that as the basis for the design concept, creating a type-only cover (p118).

As mentioned earlier, album cover imagery has come to define eras, painting a visual picture of time just as the music itself provides us with the soundtrack. Of course, influences come from trends and cultural change, what is socially acceptable, and what is popular. Either way, somebody who has paid money for a CD will take it home, open it and study every nook and cranny of the notes, lyrics, and artwork to try and find hints or clues about the musicians. Whether the designer chooses to do this using the most subtle, or the most obvious artwork and design, is not the point. As long as the consumer is able to extract information about the artist and their work from the cover, then the package has done its job.

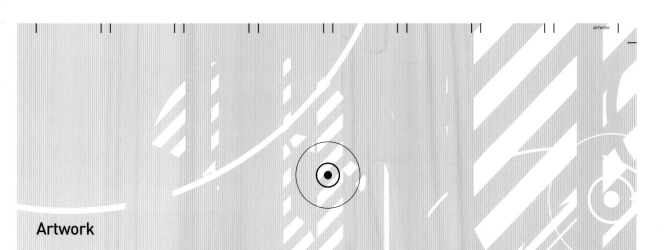

Artwork

"With CD packaging, like magazines, books etc, the design is experienced through time and interaction. Ideas can be revealed as a narrative. I don't have a problem with this. I don't want to see everything at once; I don't want to see the end of a film at the same time as the beginning"

Ian Anderson, The Designers Republic

Artist: **Abandoned Pools**
Label: **Extasy Records International**
Design: **TJ River and Todd Gallopo at Meat and Potatoes, USA**
Illustration: **TJ River**

Humanistic
The title, the lyrical themes of the album, and the artist's love of science fiction drove the concept of this package. The idea was to create an image of the artist and place him on the cover as a character in a sci-fi world. The cover image, drawn by TJ River, was based on a picture taken during a photo shoot by Flynn Larsen. It was hand-drawn then colored in Photoshop. The cover was designed to reveal the whole environment as viewed through the eyes of the artist's character. When the booklet is fully opened, a front and back view of the character is revealed on opposite sides with different views of the same "world" around him.

Artist: **Taylor Savvy**
Label: **Kitty-Yo**
Design: **Michael Tewe, Germany**
Photography: **Michael Tewe**

Ladies & Gentleman
Elegant and glamorous is how Kitty-Yo describe the dance / pop music of artist Taylor Savvy. Working on the idea of glamour, and taking inspiration from the dance aspect of the album, Michael Tewe used two models, styled them himself and did a photo shoot that resulted in the cover and some of the booklet images. A digipak was used to add to the high-quality aesthetic that the label wanted to achieve with this release.

Artist: **Eclectic Bob**
Label: **Primal Music**
Design: **Ricky Tillblad for Zion Graphics, Sweden**
Photography: **Tony Stone**

Chocolate Garden

"I had been working with about ten sketches and ideas for this," says Ricky Tillblad, "then one morning I woke up and just thought budgies, it has to be budgies. I went to my computer, visited an image bank on the internet, and there they were." The track listings and other details are styled like information design which contrasts with and complements the very kitsch imagery of the birds. A special tray card means that text can been seen from the front of the package but does not interfere with the cover image, allowing it to be text-free. Helvetica Neue typeface was used throughout.

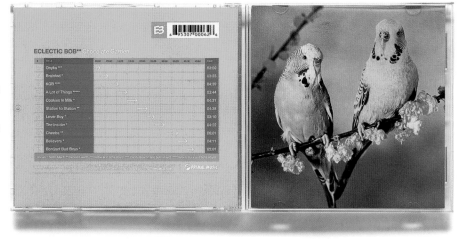

Artist: **Various**
Label: **Urban Theory**
Design: **Crush, UK**
Illustration: **Crush**

Sex, Sluts and Heaven

Crush was asked to do something pornographic with the cover of this hip hop album by various artists including The Charlatans, Jhelisa, and Nightmares on Wax. The dot-to-dot picture shown here was originally a contender for the front cover, but was thought to be too graphic. Instead it was used on the inside with a parental advisory sticker on the front. The idea comes from sketches that the artist Damien Hirst once did of himself; the designers at Crush just added the porn element. Little Dotties typeface was used thoughout to continue the dot theme.

Artist: **Jim Black with AlasNoAxis**
Label: **Winter & Winter**
Design: **Stefan Winter, Germany**
Illustration: **Yoshitomo Nara**

Splay

Artist Yoshitomo Nara's drawings, paintings, and sculptures draw on influences of childhood, both from his experiences and those of children in general. His work has graced the walls of countless galleries around the world, endearing many to the distinctive artistic style of his portraits. Typically his illustrated children either have demonic or dreamy expressions on their faces. Designers at German label Winter & Winter have reprinted Nara's artwork for the cover and the inside booklet of Splay, an album by Jim Black and his band AlasNoAxis.

Held in the same corrugated card packaging used by Winter & Winter for all its releases, Nara's sketches are laid out without text in a booklet that enables you to flick through it, just as you would a sketchbook. Nara's approach to the artwork was simple. "I already knew Jim's music well and like it very much," he explains. "I made the drawings with Jim's music playing in around two or three hours using a colored pencil, that's it." The cover image was applied using a sticker, another design feature consistent with all of Winter & Winter's releases, and the Arial typeface is debossed. The fact that a full-color Nara sketch is also printed on the disc makes for an altogether quite special CD package.

Artist: **Supergrass**
Label: **Parlophone Records**
Design: **The Designers Republic, UK**
Photography: **James Fry**

Life on Other Planets

The Designers Republic created bold
retro-style illustrations for the cover and
booklet of this Supergrass album, Life
on Other Planets. Each double page
of the uncoated stock booklet inside
features a different symmetrical print of
part photograph, part illustration images
of the band members.

Artist: **Simian**
Label: **Source Records**
Design: **Mat Maitland**
        for Big Active, UK
Art Direction: **Mat Maitland**
        for Big Active
Imagery: **Thomas Grünfeld**

One Dimension (top left)
Mr Crow (top right and bottom right)
The Wisp (bottom left)
Chemistry is What We Are
(bottom middle)

Simian's sound is both dark and uplifting
and has been described as an eerie,
dream-like alchemy of melodic vocals
and tripped-out guitars. Design and
art direction company Big Active was
commissioned to design this series of
singles and album covers that have since
won it two Music Week CAD Awards. Art
director on the project, Mat Maitland,
used the work of artist Thomas Grünfeld
on the covers; he mixed different animal
parts together to create new creatures
in the form of taxidermy sculptures.
The images are both subtle and
attention-grabbing, making for a truly
iconic series of covers.

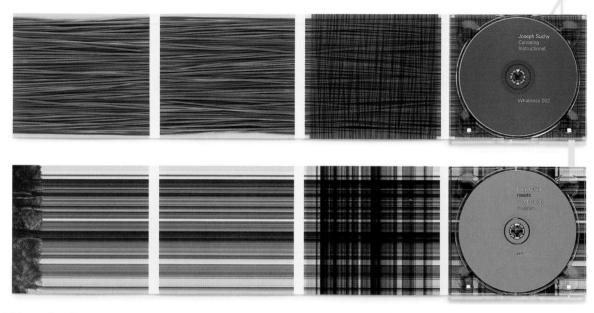

Artist: **Longpigs**
Label: **Mother Records / Polydor**
Design: **Sheridan Wall and Rob O'Connor for Stylorouge, UK**
Photography: **Nels**

Mobile Home

Film-poster photographer Nels took the photographs for the cover and booklet of this album. The shoot was done over two days in Los Angeles. The designers wanted to continue the slightly surreal narrative angle adopted on the band's previous album cover so they based the main character in the photographs (the man in the floral shirt) nominally on the character in Hunter S Thompson's book Fear and Loathing in Las Vegas. His relationship with the fish is revealed through imagery in the inserted booklet which shows him travelling around with a fish in tow that is too large for its bowl. This adds to the character's eccentricity and the surreal nature of the imagery.

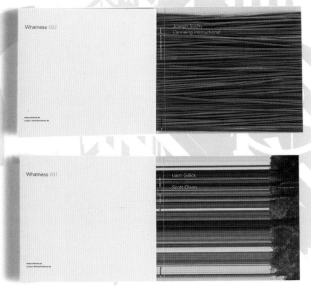

Artist:	Joseph Suchy (top)
	Liam Gillick & Scott
	Olson (bottom)
Label:	Whatness
Design:	Markus Weisbeck for
	Surface, Germany
Illustration:	Markus Weisbeck for
	Surface

Canoeing Instructional (top)
Liam Gillick meets Scott Olson
in Japan (bottom)

This music could be described as electronic but there is more to both these and other releases by this German label. The designers created an eight-panel digipak that is now used for the majority of its releases. These two examples show how the wraparound effect has been fully exploited by the artwork. On Canoeing Instructional, a stock photograph of trees was manipulated and stretched in PhotoShop to fill the whole package. Liam Gillick meets Scott Olson follows the same principle but instead of trees uses imagery of rubber bands. Production costs for these releases are far higher than if the CDs were packaged in jewel cases, but as Whatness combines many of its releases with art exhibitions, the aim is to create a treasured object rather than achieve high volume sales.

Artists:	Moder Jords Massiva
Label:	Flora&Fauna
Design:	Frans Carlqvist, Sweden
Illustration:	Frans Carlqvist

Ur Djupen

The digipak was used here because the format is closer to the feeling of a vinyl sleeve. This dub and reggae-influenced electronic album was put together by music collective Moder Jords Massiva. The lobster character on the cover was originally designed as a logo for the group. However, as this particular album was titled Ur Djupen (From the Depth) Carlqvist created an army of lobsters by multiplying the image and laying them out in rows as if they were 'emerging from the depths of the sea'.

Artist: **Underworld**
Label: **v2 / jbo**
Design: **Jason Kedgley and Dirk Van Dooren for Tomato, UK**
Photography: **Jason Kedgley and Dirk Van Dooren for Tomato**

Underworld

Design agency Tomato created this cover for Underworld. The imagery used is from a series of photographs Dirk Van Dooren produced for a Tomato exhibition at Laforet Gallery, Tokyo, in 2001. The cover image is free of the usual artist's name and album title type. Instead the text sits vertically in the spine of the jewel case in Futura Bold typeface.

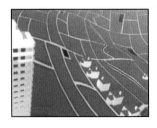

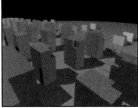

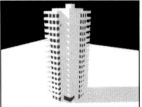

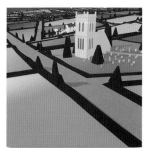

Artist: **Lemon Jelly**
Label: **XL and Impotent Fury**
Design: **Fred Deakin for Airside with Sam Burford at Transient, UK**
Illustration: **Fred Deakin**

Lost Horizons

This album cover for Fred Deakin's band Lemon Jelly makes use of a six-panel, hard-board folding cover, reminiscent of the gatefold vinyl cover, with a matt exterior and gloss interior. This album cover works on the idea that in the daytime, the countryside is glorious and the city is dull; at night the city comes to life and the countryside is dark. Sam Burford built a three-dimensional model of the countryside and city that Fred Deakin visualized in the Maya program.

Images of children on the pull-out booklet are there to "populate" the city and appear to be looking at something that the viewer can only guess at, while imagery on the inner sleeve and disc shows the three-dimensional world again from several different angles. Like the single (p29), there is no text on the cover in order to prioritize the artwork—instead a sticker was placed on the shrink-wrap for in-store recognition.

Artist: **The Promise Ring**
Label: **Jade Tree**
Design: **Jason Gnewikow at**
Public International
Illustration: **Tim Owen**
Photography: **Tim Owen**

Nothing Feels Good

Jason Gnewikow, designer at Public International, also plays guitar in The Promise Ring. He says he "wanted to create something more interesting than just a normal booklet. When you open the package, not everything is immediately revealed. You have to let your eyes sort of wander around to take the whole thing in, so it creates an experience for the viewer. Simply having to take it apart to look at it and then put it back together again creates a sort of tactile relationship between you and the package, making it less disposable." Through the artwork Gnewikow has tied two themes together: the uplifting tone of the songs,

and the melancholy feel of the lyrics. He used bright, vivid colors to convey the music with photographs of an amusement park, usually a happy experience. Upon closer examination, however, the images give a feeling of loneliness because the park is abandoned. Production was slightly expensive on this album, and because it was produced by an independent label, it had a smaller production run.

Artist: Tahiti 80
Label: **Atmosphériques /**
Minty Fresh and JVC
Design: **Laurent Fetis, France**
Artwork: **Elisabeth Arkhipoff**

Wallpaper For the Soul

This is a series of covers designed by Laurent Fetis with artwork by Elisabeth Arkhipoff. Images were commissioned especially for the album, the music of which Fetis describes as nostalgic pop. Arkhipoff has blended photography with spray-can art to produce a series of images based on the idea of nostalgia. Four different images were presented to the record company as cover options but they liked each one so much it was decided that the album should have four different covers, as shown here. Fetis used a high-quality digipak for the release so that with the booklet inside it almost feels padded. Like the package for Hideki Kaji (p111) it adds a great deal to the overall package, giving it a definite air of quality.

Artist: **The Mountain Goats**
Label: **4AD**
Design &
Art Direction: **Vaughn Oliver for v23, UK**
Design
Assistance: **Charles Grant**
Photography: **Dominic Davies**

Tallahassee

Vaughn Oliver is one of the music industry's most distinctive graphic designers and is best known for his work on releases by 4AD. This cover design for The Mountain Goats shows Oliver's response to the music on the CD and to his brief—to make the cover dark and full of vegetation. The viewer has to peel back three layers of the digipak before the final photograph is revealed, which is significantly different in tone to the rest of the package. This reflects the songs on the CD that gradually reveal the actions and outcome of a mutually destructive and dependent relationship. The cover image is of cutlery hanging in a tree in Vaughn Oliver's garden, photographed at night.

Artist: **National Skyline**
Label: **File-13 and Hidden Agenda**
Design: **Andy Mueller**
for Ohio Girl Design, USA
Photography: **Andy Mueller**

Exit Now (top)
Untitled (middle)
This=Everything (bottom)
As designer Andy Mueller explains, the
main idea of this CD series was fairly
straightforward—to try and create a
visual that looked like the CD sounds:
"The covers were inspired by the
loneliness of the music." The imagery
on each CD in this series is based on one
place or location. The inside of the first
two CDs were printed in black and white
because of budgetary constraints. This
was extended to a three-page color insert
for the band's first album Untitled. Each
package has a different series of
photographs but they relate closely to one
another in style, color, and composition.
Imagery on the covers has been allowed
to "breathe" by leaving it text-free. Type
on the disc and on the back cover is
Helvetica and Amarillo.

Artists: **Various**
Label: **A.P.C. Section Musicale**
Design: **Rik Bas Backer, France**
Photography: **Rik Bas Backer**

Manifeste

On this cover for French fashion house A.P.C., designer Rik Bas Backer (see also p124 and p139) has used photographs from a San Francisco botanical garden as a representation of the music. Manifeste is an album containing a collection of tracks that you might not expect to find together on one CD. The concept concerns botanical garden plants that are grown side-by-side in a way not found in nature. They retain a wonderfully natural quality however, just like the music. A negative detail of the cover image is printed in pink on the disc and Backer used Helvetica throughout. For the launch of the album a number of six-metre wide panoramic posters of the cover image was produced, to great effect.

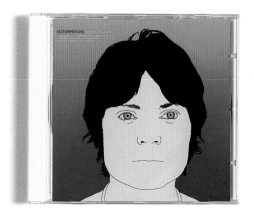

·Artist: **Motorpsycho**
Label: **Sony (Columbia)**
Design: **Kim Hiorthøy, Norway**
Illustration: **Kim Hiorthøy**

Phanerothyme

Kim Hiorthøy has designed all the covers for pop-rock band Motorpsycho's releases since the mid-90s. For the first time, this cover and booklet feature imagery of the band members, the reason being that Hiorthøy felt this was their most accessible record to date. He created the imagery in Photoshop and used Akzidenz Grotesk typeface throughout.

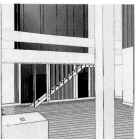

Artist: **Where Chu**
Label: **Linfair Records**
Design: **Pao & Paws, Taiwan**
Illustration: **Thomas Barwick**

Lonely City

Thomas Barwick was commissioned to draw a series of illustrations for the release of 17-year-old Taiwanese popstar Where Chu's album cover. It took three attempts as the designers wanted her to look less Taiwanese and more Chinese. Barwick was also asked to add some Western qualities to her features. Barwick does pencil sketches and then traces them in Illustrator, so that alterations such as these can easily be done on a Wacom pad. "Where Chu had just moved into a new house in a new city,

with a sense of expectation rather than loneliness. I made images of her in empty rooms which I hoped would give the minimal modernist feel that Pao wanted," explains Barwick. "I knew that it was going to be a long, pull-out format and that Pao was going to work quite freely with my Illustrator files, so I gave him as much raw material as possible in the time available. My work is influenced by Chinese and Japanese art, the simplicity of the drawing and the flat use of color; also by Western comic art and artists

from the turn of the century. To produce a portrait of a Taiwanese person in my style but with western elements was complex. Then take into account that Pao is clearly influenced by minimalist modernist designers from the West, but working in the Far East marketplace with a 21st-century client to satisfy."

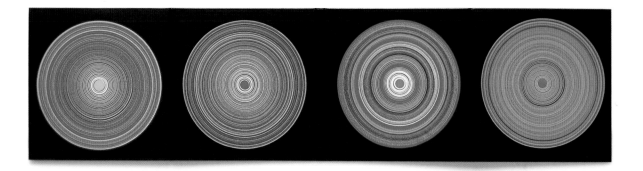

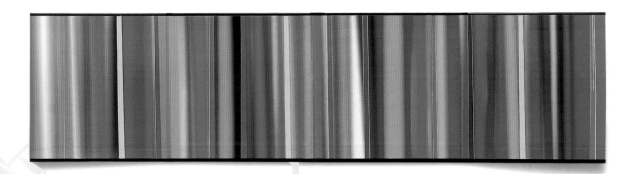

Artist: **The Music**
Label: **Virgin Records**
Design: **Linda Baritski
and Tony Perrin, UK**
Artwork: **Rob and Nick Carter**
Photography: **Tom Craig**

The Music

Rob and Nick Carter create all their work in darkness. Instead of paint and a canvas they use light and light-sensitive paper. Tony Perrin commissioned them to create four covers for The Music's first three singles. These were then used together on the album cover shown here. This series of paintings was made on a potter's wheel using Cibachrome photographic paper and a kinetic fibreoptic light. The paper is processed in the normal way and paint is then applied to the finished print. Each piece of artwork is unique. The original 24-inch works were photographed so that they could be transferred onto the cover.

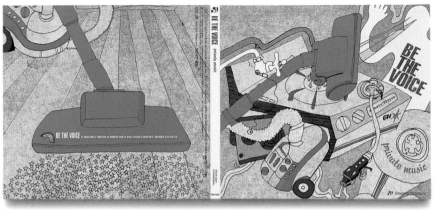

Artist: **Be The Voice**
Label: **Simplest Pleasure / Tokuma Japan Communications**
Design: **FJD (Fujita Jiro Design), Japan**
Photography: **Minoru Inoue**

Private Music

The idea of this illustrated cover is based on the album title Private Music. Designer and illustrator Jiro Fujita hand-drew these images taking inspiration from the artist's life: he lives in a very small room and goes about his daily tasks—cleaning, laundry, and so on—before he comes into contact with music. Fujita used a digipak to allow the imagery to run seamlessly around the pack.

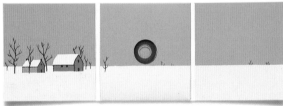

Artist: **Orange Can**
Label: **Regal Recordings**
Design: **Jeremy Plumb for Traffic, UK**
Illustration: **Jesse Cregar**

Home Burns

Jeremy Plumb wanted the illustrations here to have a depth and simplicity that related to the music. The band wanted something tactile and involving, so Plumb created this double-sided, uncoated card soft pack especially for the project. By keeping the cover fairly text-free and using a three-panel folding format, the image has the space it needs to work.

Artist: Thievery Corporation
Label: ESL Music
Design: Neal Ashby for Ashby
            Associates, USA

The Richest Man in Babylon

The songs on The Richest Man in Babylon are a down-tempo eclectic mix of jazz, reggae, bossa nova, and Middle Eastern music—all strongly rooted in a respect for the ability of human beings of all cultures and colors to find hope even in the midst of despair. This sentiment is echoed in the booklet of documentary photographs that accompany the CD. These photographs were taken by three photo-journalists—Hector Emanuel, Bill Crandall, and Daniel Cima—who were befriended by the Thievery Corporation on their travels.

"Costs grew substantially, but we tried to keep the focus on making the package work as a piece of art," says Ashby. "We all worked under the assumption that ultimately, whatever you put in will come back to you in the end. The guys felt like they had some of the best work they had ever done, and they wanted it presented in the best possible way."

Ashby purposely kept the music and imagery separate. He used a solid white jewel case as a blank canvas and created a separate booklet made with a bright white recycled stock, to contain all imagery and text, set in Helvetica Neue typeface. These two elements are held together by an O Card that features a bold, circular, target-like graphic.

"We knew the basis of the package would be photographs so we tried different covers with these images," explains Ashby. "But covers are tricky, you have to create a sort of iconic image, which generally means one simple, strong image and we felt we couldn't define the CD with one image." Instead Ashby experimented with the relationships of color and shapes to create this distinctive cover inspired by Japanese warplane insignias, 60s pop art, and Ashby's own version of what would make a good logo for a Central American freedom fighter.

Artists: **Various**
Label: **Stereo Sushi / Hed Kandi**
Design: **Zip Design, UK**
Illustration: **Zip Design**

Stereo Sushi

This is a funky underground house compilation featuring various artists released by Hed Kandi. Taking inspiration from the series title, these covers feature Zip's take on Japanese-style graphics and illustrations. Neil Bowen, Caroline Moorhouse, and David Bowden used the digipak to keep this series in line with packaging on other Hed Kandi releases. The clear plastic slip case was printed with two Pantone day-glo colors on a white base to add vibrancy. A combination of a hand-drawn logotype, Vag Rounded, Alba, and Helvetica Neue typefaces was used on the packaging.

Artist: **The White Stripes**
Label: **XL Recordings**
Design: **Jack White**
Photography: **Kevin Carraco**

Candy Cane Children

The idea for the cover imagery came from band members Meg and Jack White. "We did the shoot very quickly," explains Jack. "I just borrowed a nativity set, and made up the idea of selling Christmas cheer for $3." The stranger in the picture is the bass player from the Greenhornes. "On the back cover is an image of Meg writing '20 k+m+b 02'—an old Polish Christmas tradition that signifies the names of the three wise men. You're supposed to wipe the writing off after the feast of the epiphany I think," he says.

Artist: **No One is Innocent**
Label: **Island**
Design: **Laurent Seroussi, France**
Illustration: **Laurent Seroussi**
Photography: **Laurent Seroussi**

Utopia

Laurent Seroussi has manipulated photographs for use on the cover of this album for energetic fusion rock band No One is Innocent. Using a series of photographic portraits, he morphed them into plastic copies of themselves, giving them a computer-generated plastic covering with added lettering. The package unfolds in stages to first reveal different faces and then a fantastical map, representing some sort of utopia, in the middle. Monospace typeface was used for the text, apart from the logo which uses a typeface that Seroussi designed himself.

Artist: **Blur**
Label: **Parlophone Records**
Design: **Jeremy Plumb and Dan Poyner at Traffic, UK**
Artwork: **Julian Opie**

Blur: The Best of

This cover has become iconic; the original portraits of the band members now hang in London's National Portrait Gallery. They wanted the band on the cover as none of Blur's previous releases had done, using a style that was current. A standard CD cover was produced along with a limited edition version that had the Blur logo screen-printed onto the plastic jewel case outer and was housed inside a card slipcase. Opie won an award for Best Illustration at the 2001 UK CAD awards.

Artist: **The Black Dog**
with Black Sifichi
Label: **Hydrogen Dukebox Records**
Design: **Yacht Associates, UK**
Photography: **Tony Stone**

Unsavoury Products

Yacht Associates used a folding concertina package for this album. The music was inspired by 60s icon William Burroughs, and the package contains three postcards featuring his artwork with track listings on the reverse. Imagery of raw meat was used on the cover because designers felt that its powerful and shocking nature suited the music and its main source of inspiration.

Artist: **Brigitte Fontaine**
Label: **Virgin Records France**
Design: **Geneviève Gauckler**
and Estelle Saint
Bris, France
Illustration: **Geneviève Gauckler**

Kekeland (top)
Y'A Des Zazous (bottom)

Brigitte Fontaine is a cult artist in France, as famous for her appearance and strong personality as her music. She started singing in the 60s and these, her latest releases, feature tracks produced by Noir Désir and Sonic Youth. Although the brief was fairly open, it was important that the design would widen Fontaine's appeal to a new, young, fresh audience.

The illustration concept was of a city with a surrealist element. Graphic illustrations of guns, guitars, palm trees, flowers, animals, aeroplanes, and so on have also been used as buildings. Gauckler also designed a poster that acted as a press release for the new album.

Artist: **Gintare**
Label: **Parlophone Records**
Design: **Jeremy Plumb and Dan Poyner for Traffic, UK**
Illustration: **Andrew Cameron**
Photography: **Andrew Cameron**

Earthless (top left)
Trancenavigation (top right)
Guilty (bottom left)
Songs from Earthless (bottom right)
Traffic was asked to create the packaging for a series of promo CD singles preceding the release of Gintare's album (p49). The images were created with colored inks which were dropped into water and photographed in front of a background of the same color. The imagery was printed on a pochette and then slipped inside a transparent, colored, plastic sleeve. The actual discs are square, providing an interesting alternative.

Artist: **Bon Voyage**
Label: **BEC**
Design: **Jason Gnewikow for Public International, USA**
Illustration: **Tim Owen**
Photography: **Tim Owen**

Bon Voyage

Jason Gnewikow made this jewel case a little special by creating an interesting insert. "The only thing they came to me with was the portraits of the band," he explains. "I thought the colors were great, and also they had done these great individual shots." An uncoated stock sheet wraps around three square images of the band members that are inserted into the jewel case. Printing on a bright white uncoated stock meant the colors of the photographs, shot by Tim Owen in Seattle, are further muted. This added to the modern look that the band wanted.

Artist: **Lo Fidelity Allstars**
Label: **Skint**
Design: **Zip Design, UK**
Photography: **Dan Holdsworth**

Lo Fi's in Ibiza (top left)
Sleeping Faster (top right)
Don't Be Afraid to Love (bottom)
This set of promotional singles is for future funk band the Lo Fidelity Allstars. The promotional wallets have a large die-cut hole in the front panel. When the CD is removed, imagery that was used on the cover of the commercial releases is revealed through the hole. Dan Holdsworth did the shoot of the band on location in Yorkshire, in the north of England, which is where the band originally come from. His brief was to make the everyday look magical. Zip used the band's logotype, originally created by Red Design, and Univers Condensed for all other text and track titles.

Artist: **Stéphane Pompougnac**
Label: **Pschent**
Design: **Cedric Murac and Laurent Meszaros for WA75, France**
Photography: **Frank Sauvaire**

Hôtel Costes Quatre

Hôtel Costes is an exclusive luxury hotel in central Paris. Its compilation albums are well-known but the hotel retains a certain amount of mystery as only a privileged few have spent the night there. WA75 were commissioned to design two versions of the fourth release from Hôtel Costes: a regular and a special edition.

The packaging had to be luxurious, it had to represent the atmosphere of the hotel and increase the feeling of mystery that surrounds it. Two small, high-gloss, card posters are included in the package, along with the disc which is held in a separate card sleeve. Problems with in-store racking meant that the original dimensions of the box had to be altered in order for it to fit the larger stores' systems. Helvetica Neue typeface was used throughout.

Artists:	Various
Label:	Subetage Records
Design:	Christoph Steinegger at Büro X, Germany
Photography:	Henning Bock

Putinout

This cover was created for a compilation album by Russian artists after the Kursk disaster in 2000. The brief was to highlight the dramatic situation in Russia. The cover features a model of the Kursk in a bottle of vodka signifying the political powerlessness of the Russian music scene under Putin. "The reactions were mainly positive since finally someone said something," explains Steinegger, "but it also caused quite a stir."

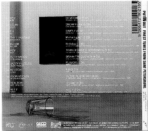

Artist:	Basement Jaxx
Label:	XL Recordings
Art Direction:	Mat Maitland and Gerard Saint
Design:	Mat Maitland for Big Active, UK
Illustration:	Mat Maitland, Rob Kidney, and René Habermacher

Get Me Off

Mat Maitland designed and created all the imagery for Basement Jaxx's single covers in conjunction with René Habermacher, who produced the airbrushed images. Rob Kidney produced the graffiti for the covers. "This imagery was very much an extension of the 'defaced very slick' theme we developed for the album campaign. This time the theme is much more sexual in nature, and goes right back to some of the original visuals we showed the band when the album was still in progress," explains Kidney.

Artist: **Ugress**
Label: **Port Azur / Tuba**
Design: **Sopp Collective, Australia**
Illustration: **Sopp Collective**

Loungemeister

The concept for this single cover came from the aesthetic of the video that the collective had previously made for Ugress's track Loungemeister. The brief for the video was open; the main idea was to play on the legendary stardom of 80s rock with the story of the video taking place in a small town in Norway. The overall style is based on computer game graphics from the same time. Sopp created a strong link to the video by using its imagery: the picture of the town and a classic cheesy band shot. These images were applied to a poster which when folded became the CD cover. Hand-drawn pixel fonts were created specially for the project.

Artist: **Kristofer Åström
           and Hidden Truck**
Label: **V2, Startracks**
Design: **Henrik Walse for Walse
           Custom Design, Sweden**
Illustration: **Jonas Banker for
           Banker Wessel**

Connected (left)
Northern Blues (right)

Åström wanted images of the band in the booklet and some reference to his home in the north of Sweden. Banker created portraits using a stencil and spray can which were hand-cut; in most cases it took two per person to get the darker and lighter imagery. A limited run of 2000 covers was produced using a gatefold digipak; the rest were jewel cases.

Artists: **Various**
Label: **EMI Records**
Design: **Jeremy Plumb for Traffic, UK**

ESound 01
ESound 05

This is the second series of promotional EMI releases designed by Traffic. The covers are based on the design principles of the first (p111) but the designers used slightly different packaging: a lancing pack with a soft plastic outer. Also, illustrators rather than photographers were used, including Vault49, Sarah Howell, Cody Hudson, Marion Deuchars, and Alan Baker. Each release has a unique color in order to brand the series and the artists' details screen-printed onto the outer cover for prominence.

Artist: **The Charlatans**
Label: **Island / Universal Records**
Design: **Gerard Saint for Big Active, UK**
Art Direction: **Gerard Saint**
Photography: **Tom Sheenan and Sinisha Nisevic (fans)**

Live It Like Love It

Simple yet sophisticated, the inserted concertina-folded, image-only booklet was duotone-printed in black and silver on gloss stock, and features pictures of the band and its fans. The finishing touch is a sticker in the form of a backstage pass stuck on to the cover of the CD with the album's title, Live It Like You Love It, and a handwritten date on each.

Artist:	**Heather Nova**
Label:	**Sony**
Design:	**Nicolai Schaanning Larsen for St Paulus, Norway**
Illustration:	**Nicolai Schaanning Larsen for St Paulus**

Oyster

The imagery on this cover is described by the designer as a celebration of the music inspired by nature, flowers, and organic forms. A CD, double EP, and a number of promotional posters were produced using this artwork.

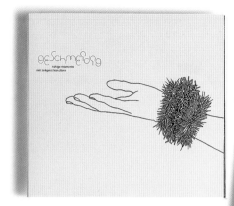

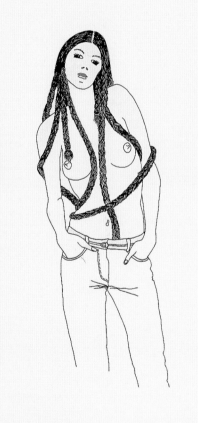

Artists: **Various**
Label: **Polydor Zeitgeist /
Universal Music**
Design: **Eike König, Germany**
Illustration: **Stepha Schede**

Geschmeidig

Stepha Schede created the illustrations for this German electronic compilation album entitled Geschmeidig. Different images by Schede are revealed as the viewer opens the package; the idea being that once the artwork is pieced together it forms a story. The designers wanted to use an unvarnished card for the package but the budget did not allow for this. However, the package retains the sense of quality demanded by using simple illustrations, an interesting card-based package, and a specially designed font.

Artist: **Russell Haswell**
Label: **MEGO**
Design: **Russell Haswell, Austria**
Photography: **Wolfgang Tillmans**

Live Salvage 1997–2000

The artist Russell Haswell designed his own cover using spot varnish to apply the text, a wipe-clean stock on the digipak, and an image of him DJing at a party in London taken by photographer Wolfgang Tillmans who just happened to be there. The cover design is an appropriate reflection of the music inside and carries a subtle air of cool, understated design.

Artists:	Various
Label:	EMI Records
Design:	Jeremy Plumb and Dan Poyner for Traffic, UK
Photography:	Alan Clarke, Harry Gruyaert, and Martin Rose

You're Keeping Me Up All Night
(right)
I Wish You Could Be Here With Me
(far right)
Jump On Board, Take a Ride
(bottom right)

This is the first series of compilation promotional releases by EMI Records in the UK designed by Traffic. The CDs contain tracks by various artists signed to the label and act as sampler CDs for promotional use. Traffic sourced and used various photographers for the series applying imagery onto stickers and then the stickers to uncoated card covers. As with the plastic-covered series (p108) each release has a different color band printed to differentiate it. Rounded Helvetica was used throughout.

Artist:	Hideki Kaji
Label:	Trattoria
Design:	Laurent Fetis, France
Illustration:	Laurent Fetis
Photography:	Laurent Fetis

You Will Love Me

Laurent Fetis (see also p92) is best-known for his work for French band Mellow, whose last two album covers and countless singles feature his unmistakably bold, colorful and graphic illustrations. Through imagery only, both on the Hideki Kaji cover and within the booklet, Fetis created a narrative based around the idea of Kaji at a garden party. "My brief was to recreate a US college atmosphere," says Fetis, who was influenced by the panoramic paintings of Alex Katz.

Artist : Compilation by Barry 7
Label: Lo Recordings
Design: Kjell Ekhorn and Jon Forss
for Non-Format, UK
Illustration: Kjell Ekhorn and Jon Forss
for Non-Format

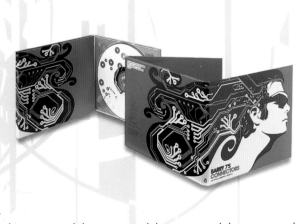

Connectors
Connectors 2

These albums contain 60s and 70s music from French and Italian libraries compiled by artist Barry 7. The first is mostly avant-garde electronica, and the latter has a more orchestral movie soundtrack bias. Barry 7 showed the designers his sketchbook of images from 60s and 70s magazines and catalogs.

"We found some illustrations used on gift boxes from the late 60s, which were the inspiration for the hair shape and the idea of using a profile image. We decided to illustrate Barry 7 with his trademark Karl Lagerfeld sunglasses and to transform his hair into an intricate, organic circuit board image," explains Forss. "We were keen to make sure the lines had a slightly rough and awkward quality, as we wanted it to look as though it could have been produced in the late 60s."

The first compilation, Connectors, was printed in black and red. The second was black on avocado green, and the image is flipped, so that when the two albums are placed side-by-side the two Barrys face each other. Both CDs are packaged in six-panel digipaks made of white reverse card. This kind of pulp card has a smooth and a rough side; the designers chose to print on the rough side for an added tactile quality. A circuit board design was printed on the CD, white on white, i.e. a white base ink was printed first to cover the surface of the CD (apart from the circular holes in the design). It was then overprinted in a matt white ink. The result has great subtlety, particularly in the differing texture of the glossy base white and the rougher matt white inks.

Avant Garde bold typeface was used for the headline text and Vectrex for the rest. Vectrex is produced by Swiss type foundry Lineto, and is based on the vector fonts designed for early video games such as Asteroids. Connectors 2 has a grid layout inside to suggest early computer dot matrix printers, where a space would often be printed with another character—in this case an asterisk.

"Music has always been an extraordinary trigger for ideas so the very first stage in the packaging process is to listen to the music"

Jon Forss, Non-Format

Founders of Anglo-Scandinavian design house EkhornForss / Non-Format, Kjell Ekhorn and Jon Forss collaborate on print design projects for the music and publishing industries. One of their most renowned packaging designs involved a Hoover bag stuffed with fluff for a project for Sonic Youth guitarist Thurston Moore in 2000 (p137). They also art direct and design The Wire magazine.

What inspires you when designing an album cover?
Music has always been an extraordinary trigger for ideas so the very first stage in the packaging process is to listen to the music. Photography, fine art, fashion, and architecture all play their part. It's always nice when an idea comes to us, and it's all the more rewarding when it can be used on a piece we are working on right away. A good idea can come from anywhere, but it's being able to recognize one when it comes that's the real thrill.

How important do you think an album cover is?
The front cover design has to do most of the selling but someone once said that "to suggest is to create, to describe is to destroy." This is a principle we often apply when designing as it's often more satisfying if there's more to the packaging than just the front cover image. This way a design's main idea can be hidden inside and only hinted at on the exterior. With more and more independent labels being bought by the big labels, more and more designers have to adhere to a list of corporate rules and regulations. However, strong creativity will usually find a way of bending rules and finding new ways of expression.

Do you think CDs can be made as desirable, or collectable as vinyl?
CDs are already collectable. Whether they are as collectable as vinyl is impossible to say. I collect CDs not because of the format but because of some special quality that draws me in. Designers should always be looking for new ways to package these 12cm discs. I'm sure it's only a matter of time before the 12cm disc is replaced by something else entirely, but in the meantime...

What would you cite as the major differences between mainstream and independent labels?
There seems to be a greater and greater divide between mainstream music and independent underground music.

Mainstream music has many more systems in place channelled to selling it: there is more exposure on TV, movies, and radio than for underground music; record companies can afford huge, dominating displays in record stores. Experimental underground music has a harder job of getting noticed so the sleeves are often the only clue as to the kind of music on the disc. These sleeves have to be more interesting and experimental; they have to work a little harder in order to compete.

What do you most enjoy about designing an album cover?
The design and the music often get very strongly associated with one another. We try to alter or enhance people's perception of the music in some way. As art directors and designers of The Wire, we sometimes get promo copies of albums with a blank sleeve and it's always interesting to see the final packaged version of these same albums in the shops. It's like meeting someone for the first time having only ever spoken to them on the phone before, and finally putting a face to a voice.

And the future?
With more and more music being sold over the Internet, the designer's job is bound to shift. It's important for us to produce packaging that people want to take home with them.

London, 2002

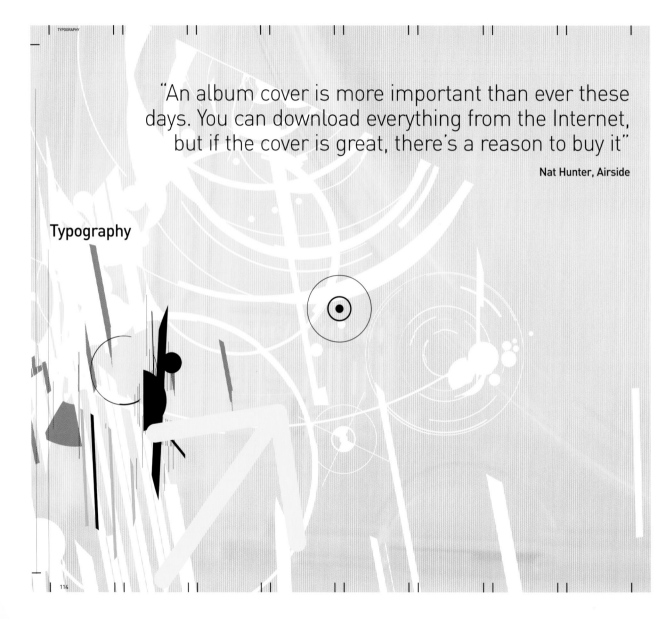

"An album cover is more important than ever these days. You can download everything from the Internet, but if the cover is great, there's a reason to buy it"

Nat Hunter, Airside

Typography

Artists:	**Compilation by Michel Gaubert and Marie Branellec**
Label:	**Colette**
Design:	**Work in Progress, France**

Various—Colette

Featuring the likes of Beck, Chicks on Speed, and Felix Da Housecat, Michel Gaubert, who compiled this series of compilation CDs for French fashion house Colette, describes them as "a sign of the times." Ezra Petronio kept the design simple by maximizing the minimalist effect of the transparent jewel case by adding only one-color, screen-printed Helvetica type onto each cover. To emphasize the series, Petronio has repeated a basic graphic solution on each package but brought subtle changes to each to differentiate them. The most obvious change is the color, but the use of varying typographic layouts created by combining the type on the case with the type on the disc also adds to the individuality of each CD. For Colette No1,

white type sitting over a solid white disc forces the viewer to remove the CD to read the text. The black Colette No2 is designed to create a moiré effect if the CD is not properly aligned in its case. All the information on the blue Colette No4 is split between the case and the CD so both elements must combine to make the information readable. The typographic layout here is typical of Work in Progress' style, another strong example of which is its cover for Fischerspooner (p116).

Artist: **Fischerspooner**
Label: **Ministry of Sound**
Design: **Work in Progress, France**
Photography: Roe Ethridge

Fischerspooner#1

Fischerspooner (see also p115), a performance art duo, uses music as one of its many media of expression that also include film, video, and photography. Hailing from the USA, their special effect-filled stage show extravaganzas that fuse electronic pop, conceptual art, and outrageous costumes, have created waves both in the USA and in Europe.

Work in Progress designed an unusual CD package for the duo's genre of music. "The aim was to draw on how the duo mocks the banality and monotony of electronic pop culture by blatantly exploiting it," explains Ezra Petronio, creative director. "To suit the irony, we designed the entire visual identity using a compilation of quotes from various magazines as well as inventing some too."

Petronio treated the upper-case type as imagery, using a variety of point sizes and a family of ten typefaces. When opened, the matt-coated, six-panel digipak allows the full extent of the design to be appreciated, making it look like a banner. A twelve-page booklet inside also sees unusual typography and an eclectic mix of typefaces, all of which sit neatly inside an O card.

Artist: **Muslimgauze**
Label: **Soleilmoon Recordings**
Design: **Alexander Baumgardt,**
Germany

Hummus (left)
Veiled Sisters Remix [right]

The focus and inspiration of experimental electronic artist Muslimgauze is the sound and culture of the Middle East. He uses samples of Middle Eastern music when producing tracks and, by mixing them with hard electronic beats, he removes the original rationale, taking the music somewhere completely different by placing it in an unusual context. Baumgardt wanted to convey that idea visually.

"I ended up with the Sufi culture and its Rumi poetry," explains Baumgardt. "Sufi culture is similar to Buddhism in that its highest goal is enlightenment through love and consciousness. I have related the Rumi poetry excerpts to a typographic grid in a similar way to how Muslimgauze relates his audio samples to a time grid— a common electronic music technique."

The result is a reduced yet dynamic visual expression in which the words and sentences, set in Helvetica Neue, can be read as fragments or as a whole and even in different directions; similarly the music can be heard and experienced in different ways.

As waves upon my head
the circling curl,
So in the sacred dance
weave ye and whirl
Dance then, O heart,
a whirling circle
be.

Muslimgauze
Hummus

I became filthy water,
roadside trash,
take me from this path
and get me
home.

Muslimgauze
Veiled Sisters Remix

Artist: **Hattler**
Label: **Universal / Polydor**
Design: **Karlssonwilker Inc., USA**

No Eats Yes

Between them Karlssonwilker Inc. created one black element, or shape, every day for four weeks for this modern pop album by Hattler. It has resulted in quite a graphic, type-based cover that features boxed Spartan typeface. The sticker on the front cover hides the photograph of the artist underneath that is revealed when the booklet is removed. Universal / Polydor, who produced the CD, thought their existing machines would be able to apply the sticker, but they couldn't, so students were hired at the last minute to apply them by hand.

CITY ROCKERS PRESENT FUTURISM 2.

Article 2. Section 1 (a).
Redressing the balance, claiming back from the past and the future the incentive in its purist form Musically a progression from its original, microcosmic enclave (futurism one, section 1a) it can be comparable to that split second of tranquillity before everything goes off. The 808 snare snap snapping faster and faster, with a Synth enthused Der Da Da Da Da reverberating around your eardrums, the hair standing up on the back of your neck as you catch your reflection a thousand times over in the glitter-ball. Wrestled away from the sweaty palms of the navel gazing minority it's swallow diving on the dance floor. It's Aggit-pop thrust back into the hands of the rightful multitude (See Appendix section 3, Cityrocks5CD)

Artists:	**Various**
Label:	**City Rockers**
Design:	**David Smith for Milk, UK**
Art Direction:	**David Smith for Milk**
Writer:	**Matthew Gibbins for Milk**

Futurism 1
Futurism 2

The music of Futurism was defined in its press and poster campaign as "6.25% House, 12.5% Electronica, 28.125% Punkelectro, 12.5% Techno and 40.625% Electro." Working closely with a writer and City Rockers, the designers created a dictionary definition of what Futurism was and what it stood for. This text then became the basis of the cover applied to the first and second releases in Helvetica Heavy and Clarendon typefaces respectively. The solid-colored jewel cases used colors that were not normally associated with music, hence the pink and green. Unlike other compilation albums, the Futurism releases do not list the artists, and feature no photography or illustration.

Artist:	**The Foo Fighters**
Label:	**RCA Records**
Design:	**Brett Kilroe and Robin Hendrickson at RCA Records, USA**
Illustration:	**Raymond Pettibon**

Singles from the ONE BY ONE album

The idea for these cover images came from band member Dave Grohl. Grohl chose artwork by Raymond Pettibon, a fine artist, who created classic album art for early punk rock bands such as Black Flag and the Minutemen, as well as Sonic Youth's major label debut, Goo. The heart images used here were both preexisting and those created by Pettibon for the band. The artist's own ink and brush writing is the principal type for the logo and titles. Futura and Times New Roman were secondary to create a quiet and unobtrusive second voice.

Artist: 'S Rankler Chörle
Label: Gebhard Mathis Records
Design: Peter Felder for Felder
            Grafikdesign, Austria

Himmelslichter (Heaven Lights)

Based on a composition from Laurentius von Schnifis, this CD consists of a 40-person chorus singing gospel and traditional spiritual songs. Using the album title as the main point of reference, designer Peter Felder experimented with printing typography onto transparent paper to give the impression of lights fading beyond fog, clouds, or a dawn mist: "I wanted to make the title light and mystic, like the music," explains Felder. "The idea comes out of the music, form follows sound." When the booklet is fully open, the letters appear back to front and in no legible order; when closed they form complete words. The tray card is made from the same stock, the full effect of which can be seen when the case is held up to the light. The paper stock is 135gsm transparent paper which added very little extra production cost.

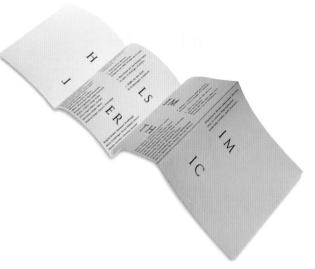

Artist: **Minus**
Label: **Smekkleysa / Bad Taste**
Design: **Gunnar Thor Vilhjalmsson, Iceland**
Photography: **Borkur Sigthorsson**

Jesus Christ Bobby

According to Gunnar Thor Vilhjalmsson, Icelandic band Minus play a fusion of hardcore metal and experimental noise. It is this that he and Borkur Sigthorsson wanted to get across here. Sterile imagery was combined with raw and randomly laid out handwritten text on the UV-coated booklet. "We wanted each word to be unique, so we got two friends to write all the lyrics with variable styles," says Vilhjalmsson. "The rules were to use random styles where appropriate, and when you made a mistake, instead of erasing it you should write over it," he adds. "Then I took the whole lot, cut it down, picked out what I wanted to use and kind of puzzled it all together."

Artist: **Jake Mandell**
Label: **Carpark Records**
Design: **Todd Hyman, USA**

The Placekick EP

Todd Hyman founded Carpark Records in 1999. Musical styles range from ambient to the techno / experimental electronics of Jake Mandell. Hyman designed this minimalist CD package for Mandell's The Placekick EP, part of the Sports Fan series.

Hyman used a FAN-CD—a regular 5-inch diameter plastic CD but with sound only on the inner 3 inches, leaving an outer clear band of 2 inches. "I used a FAN-CD because then you can print all types of interesting shapes on it," explains Hyman. "If I used a 3-inch disc I would be more limited. By using a FAN-CD I could have extra space to work with and so hide the metal portion of the CD." He chose to lay out the type on a clear plastic because he thought it was "visually stunning" and not something he had seen before. It has been printed twice—the right way round,

and back to front—so that the album name, track listings and details can be read from the front or back to allow for the lack of booklet and cover.

Being an independent label there were budgetary constraints so Hyman printed the 1500 tray cards at a high-street copy shop, two to a sheet, then cut each one out by hand. Although this was a low budget production, the clean, sophisticated, and almost clinical design makes for a CD package that suits the music inside perfectly.

Artists: **Various**
Label: **Ritornell**
Design: **Alorenz, Germany**

Ritornell series Nos 5, 6, 7 and 8

Shown here are six covers from a series of albums designed by Angela Lorenz for Ritornell, a Force Inc. sub-label. Like her other work, and in line with the music on the CDs, the design is fairly minimal. The concept uses typographic characters such as + → - to replace the blank space between letters, thus dissolving the usually obvious distinction between foreground (information) and background (white space). The characters used to do this change with each release, as do the colors, in order to differentiate one from another.

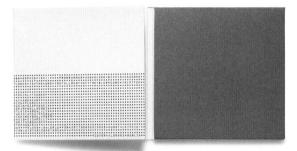

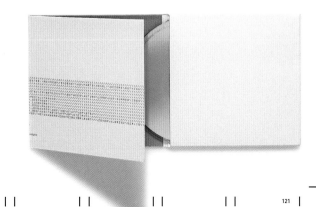

Artist:	**AMFM**
Label:	**Polyvinyl Records**
Design:	**Phillip Dwyer for Apt13, USA**
Illustration:	**Phillip Dwyer for Apt13**

Getting into Sinking

The typefaces used on this album are a combination of hand-drawn types, and fonts that appear to be hand-drawn, used to get a sense of intimacy across. The pictures, commissioned specially for the album, are of the primary band members on the beach. "The idea was tangibility," comments Dwyer. "I thought the photographs were very ethereal and it was nice to 'muck them up' with gritty type. Like these are just two guys you, or anybody, could know or see walking down the street. I tried to convey that by having candid photography coupled with a mostly hand-drawn typographic style. Maybe it can be seen as a journal of two friends." There was no template for the design as such, instead Dwyer crammed the text throughout the booklet as if someone was trying to get as much information onto this small piece of paper as possible.

Artist:	**Merzbow / Jazzkammer**
Label:	**Smalltown Supersound**
Design:	**Rune Mortensen, Norway**
Photography:	**Lasse Marhaug**

Live at Molde International Jazz Festival

As it says on the cover, this album was recorded live when artists Merzbow and Jazzkammer played at the Molde International Jazz Festival. However, the music of Merzbow and Jazzkammer is not—as you might think from the style of the cover—jazz; but rather experimental electronic music. Oslo-based designer, Rune Mortensen used the circumstances in which this recording was made as a basis for his design, applying a style more commonly associated with another musical genre to the cover. The use of subtle colors, simple layout, and large DIN typeface is unmistakably based on a simple typographic design that is now synonymous with jazz albums; the uncluttered layout of which also reflects the minimalist nature of the music inside.

Artist: Doktor Kosmos
Label: NONS / MNW
Design: Sweden Graphics, Sweden
Illustration: John Gripenholm
Photography: John Gripenholm

Eva's Story (top)
Le Punkrocker (bottom)

These two covers are for the release of Doktor Kosmos' first single (bottom) and album (top). Designers at Sweden Graphics were asked to create open-minded and communicative covers; the band had a message to give its listeners and the design was to make this clear. Color was kept to a minimum on the text-heavy, graphic covers to give the copy clarity. The designers chose to print all the cover information onto stickers, which were then applied to the solid white jewel cases. A pull-out poster, which comes with the album, features a photograph of the band on one side and all the lyrics on the other, styled as a more colorful version of the cover.

The tracks on the album work like a rock opera, in that the songs are linked by a story. Large arrows link the lyrics of each song so that the listener can follow the story. Small images that relate to the story also feature on the poster. Ziggurat and Helvetica typefaces have been used thoughout (see also p124).

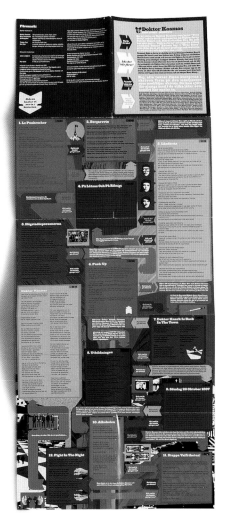

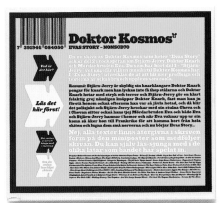

Artist: **Doktor Kosmos**
Label: **NONS / MNW**
Design: **Sweden Graphics, Sweden**
Illustration: **Sweden Graphics**

Fyra Nya Filmer and Reportage

Here is another cover designed by Sweden Graphics for Doktor Kosmos (see also p123), again with a heavy typographic presence. This digipak EP features photography from one of the band's live concerts and a sticker, applied by hand, containing all the information in badly typed Futura. The idea was to create a fast and messy look without giving a token punk sense, so still maintaining a strong feel of design. The jewel case contains nine unbound sheets of paper, printed mainly in black and white, some in red, that when folded make a 36-page booklet. The designers wanted the listener to be able to spread them out and for them to feel more like small posters than pages. It is made from a paper stock more commonly used for subway billboard posters so that they could fit the maximum possible amount of pages in. Sweden Graphics also found that the stock forced the design to look fast and furious.

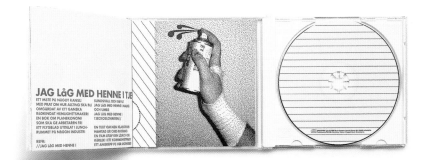

Artists: **Various**
Label: **A.P.C. Section Musicale**
Design: **Rik Bas Backer, France**
Illustration: **Rik Bas Backer**
Photography: **Rik Bas Backer**

Ignore the Beat

Rik Bas Backer's (see also p95 and p139) application of bold Gothic Letter typeface onto this Ignore the Beat disc ensures recognition in and out of its jewel case. There is no booklet, and consequently no cover, so the type on the disc has to compensate. Ignore the Beat is one of successful French fashion house A.P.C.'s latest dance releases, comprising an eclectic mix of musical genres including trance, disco, and techno. Backer combined strong and direct typography with bold abstract imagery to reflect the musical style, using three contrasting typefaces that work surprisingly well together. "None of the elements really fit, they just work together," he says. "I like the unexpected effect of all the elements. 'Effect' is really the key to this design."

Artist: **Herbert**
Label: **Soundslike**
Design: **Sarah Hopper, UK**
Illustration: **Sarah Hopper**

Bodily Functions

The music on this album is British house with a jazz influence. Sarah Hopper was given an open brief for the packaging design and asked simply to create something that she felt was appropriate for the music. Hopper used type to form imagery on the cover and inside with Akzidenz Grotesk Black. "I like using type as imagery," explains Hopper. "Type is part of the composition anyway, so why not take it a little further rather than just trying to fit it into a spare bit of space." The artist asked that the song lyrics be on the disc as he liked the idea of the listener not being able the read the words while playing the CD, therefore making the reading and listening two separate activities. The digipak was two-color printed while the vinyl version was four-color. Hopper created a design that is just as effective using both printing processes.

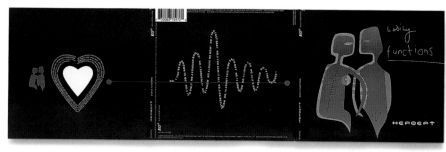

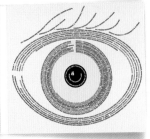

Artist: **Scott Fields**
Label: **Cri / Blueshift**
Design: **Karlssonwilker Inc., USA**

96 Gestures

Without the hot-stamped blue lines, the front and the back of this pack would be exactly the same. The lines simply eliminate different text on each side, revealing the artists' names on the front, and track listings, times and so on, on the back. This type of double-opening jewel case packaging is rarely seen, perhaps because there are so many other, more aesthetically pleasing options available. However, Karlssonwilker have played with this format cleverly, making an interesting typographic cover that enhances the three-dimensional quality of the package.

Artist: Brooks
Label: Mantis Recordings
Design: Rob Coke for twelve:ten, UK
Illustration: Rob Coke for twelve:ten

You, Me & Us

Brooks produces underground deep house music. For this album cover he gave Rob Coke, then at twelve:ten, an old picture from a menswear catalog to be used as a starting point for the artwork. Inside the digipak is a montage of travel ephemera including a boarding pass and hotel receipt. "I was attempting to reproduce the kind of montage you'd find in a 70s concept album, or a live LP that featured ticket stubs and ephemera," explains Coke. "The gatefold opening effect was ideal for this. The idea was to reveal a little more of the characters on the inside, and to trace an imaginary evening through the stuff they collect: tickets, weird Polaroids, receipts. They are familiar items but are given a slightly other-worldly twist."

Artist: Fila Brazillia
Label: 23
Design: David McSherry, UK

We Build Arks

Fila Brazillia produce music that could be described as surreal R&B. One of its members, David McSherry, designed this cover for the release of We Build Arks, taking inspiration from memories of building an Airfix model of The Ark Royal. "I always liked the big butch letters and numbers on the sides of those sinister gray machines," he explains. "Their aesthetic is an accident, they're designed to be functional and gray. I wanted the sleeve to be the same." McSherry used Machine typeface and then outlined each letter in white in Quark. An illustration of a battleship features on the disc with a personalized code on the side—FB23.

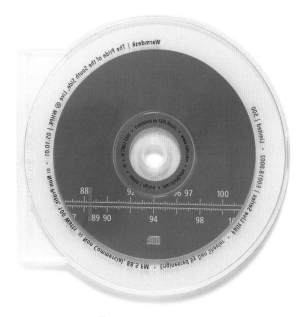

Artist:	Stephan Mathieu and Warm Desk
Label:	Fällt
Design:	Fehler, UK
Illustration:	Fehler

Gigue, Live @ A-Musik (left)
The Pride of the South Side, Live @ WHPK (right)

Christopher Murphy attends many gigs which is where the idea for the Fällt Live Series came from, as he wanted to preserve some of the more memorable performances. Sony DADC produce a CD format whereby text can be printed on both sides which Fällt used for this cover, putting all the information on the CD itself. The transparent outer edge of the disc allows for imagery and text to be printed on both sides. The soft, flexible transparent plastic C-Shell is a widely available packaging format. Each release is represented by a different color to give it its own identity. The artist suggested the Duran Duran quote on the yellow CD because the music is derived from Duran Duran's Drive By. The radio dial on the other CD reflects the fact that it was a live radio performance.

"As a company we have become more interested in all the other parts of the industry: video, web design, and so on, because I think that is where it is going"

Rob O'Connor, Stylorouge

Rob O'Connor founded renowned UK design house Stylorouge over 20 years ago after leaving the art department of Polydor in the early 80s. He has worked with a wide variety of artists on album covers. O'Connor and his team are now mastering other creative aspects of the industry, including web design and video production.

How do you think the music industry has changed since you began designing 25 years ago?
In the last two years the whole industry has gone mad; it is being completely dictated to by radio and retail. Radio on the basis that if a record isn't played on certain stations, record companies see no point in releasing it. Retail on the basis that stores are polarizing and the organizations are becoming much bigger. A lot of the independent stores are going out of business and the small chains are having a hard time. Consequently if you're a small artist on an independent label without big marketing or the clout to allow chains to make price reductions, you are just not going to get in-store. Even if you do, you're unlikely to be discounted; you don't stand much of a chance.

How have you adapted to these changes?
As a company we have become more interested in the other parts of the industry: video, web design and so on, because I think that is where it is going. When it becomes conventional for people to buy their music from the web, whether it is in a cover, on a disc, or just downloaded, there will still be a demand for imagery and other "value-added" elements. Hopefully this won't be accompanied by the existing boring retail-focused constraints —price labels dictating the position of typography for example.

What is the difference between mainstream and independent?
Mainstream companies can afford to sell records to people who don't buy many. Hardcore music fans look for records on small labels, on import, in shops, online, wherever. And they might buy 50 to 100 a year, if they can afford it. The more interesting bands are catered for by the independents on all levels: dance, jazz, folk, whatever. Although the smaller labels don't have money, they are more open to creativity. That's not a cheap slight at the major companies, they are also capable of being creative, but their wings are clipped by convention and market forces.

Do you think CD covers will ever be as collectable as the old vinyl format?
I hope so, and I think that can only be made possible by a combination of creative thinking from the producers, manufacturers, the record companies, and public perception. By working together, I have a theory that CD packaging could reflect the system adopted by books. You can have your "hardback" CD that comes out maybe a week or two earlier, and for a little extra cash you get a really nice bound cover, maybe with extra pages and so on. Then a couple of weeks later you get the cheaper version for the people who just want the music and not all the peripherals.

And the future?
We are told that over the last couple of years, sales of pop music have dropped, not because the product is no good but because people are getting music off the Internet. I think the experience of buying CDs is not enough of a seductive experience and until this is improved, the downturn will continue.

London, 2002

"Some bands I've worked with don't feel like their record is real unless it's in a jewel case"

The Client: Tim Stedman, MCA Records

Tim Stedman is vice president and creative director of MCA Records, Santa Monica, USA. He has been working in the music industry for over ten years and has designed covers for many bands including blink-182, Richard Buckner, and Lyle Lovett.

How many of the decisions about album cover artwork are based on the marketability of it rather than the design aesthetic?
In the current climate I think marketability may be somewhat prioritized.

Do you think there is enough creativity within CD cover design?
I think there is plenty of creativity, it's the limitations of business that often stifle it.

What do you think about the jewel case as a packaging product?
I see the jewel case as a format like anything else—it has advantages and disadvantages. When it makes sense to use that format, you just need to do the best job you can within that. Some bands I've worked with don't feel like their record is real unless it's in a jewel case.

Do you think it is a good thing that the main bulk of artwork on a CD package is inside?
I think it's nice to have a surprise left after you've bought the record. From a design point of view I guess it means you had better make sure what you put on the outside is what you'd like communicated first. The alternative that would allow consumers to see the artwork would be to not shrink-wrap the records, but that would probably create a problem for retailers.

What do you most enjoy about designing for the CD format and why?
I really love musicians and music and feel honored to be the person helping to create the package for them.

Santa Monica, 2002

04

"Designing something that suits the music is
the number one priority, otherwise you have
failed no matter how good it looks"

David Nakamoto, Multifresh

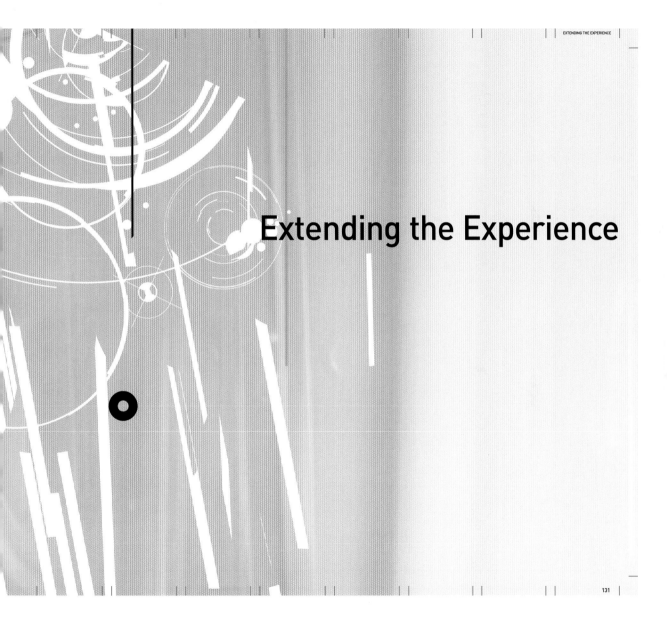

Extending the Experience

"There is some very interesting packaging for CDs, so if people can provide the budgets for these there is a lot of scope for collectable pieces"

Hamish Makgill, Red Design

Introduction

The CD package is not only limited to being a listening experience. When given the opportunity, designers have found many ways in which to extend the consumer's experience, from changing the inserted booklet into a full-blown book, to the inclusion of computer-readable imagery on the disc. It is not just stickers and badges these days. This chapter explores the many methods that designers use to bring more to the CD than just music.

The reasons for doing this are varied, but due to the increase in costs incurred when manufacturing anything other than the standard format it tends to mainly be for promotional reasons. Artist Amy Studt's cloth-covered CD book (p134), designed by Root, was a promotional CD package for the launch of her debut single. As an unknown artist her label wanted packaging that would get the attention of radio DJs, magazine editors, and so on, to encourage them to play or review the single. Of course the packaging alone did not make this single a hit, but in the tough and competitive environment of pop it can help set an artist apart.

Designer Rudy VanderLans, head of the US label Émigré, but perhaps better known as editor of Émigré magazine, has designed and produced some classic pieces of CD packaging in recent years. Production costs have been higher, but as a designer he appreciates the aesthetic values as much as the musical values of a CD, perhaps more than a record company executive. His Dreaming Out Loudest boxed series has included mini pillows, feathers, and a 72-page book (p149) in an attempt to titillate all the senses and extend the user experience.

In addition to the physical it has become usual for CD singles to include screensavers or desktop imagery, and increasingly a digital version of the single video. It is an attempt by record companies to both increase sales and extend the experience of the consumer. With the increasing popularity of the MP3, such extras on CDs encourage people to continue to buy hard copies of music. With the opportunity to bring sound, interaction, printed text, and imagery together in one neat and compact object, each CD package has the potential to become its own multimedia universe.

Extending the Experience

"The most fun part is the conception, everything
is open and you can dream a little bit"

Frank Fenstermacher, Ata Tak

Artist: **Amy Studt**
Label: **Polydor**
Design: **Root, UK**
Photography:**Nazarin Montag
and Clare Muller**

Just a Little Girl

Christopher Ringsell at Root designed this promotional book for the release of Amy Studt's debut single, Just a Little Girl. The book is held in a cloth cover from an uncoated stock interspersed with Transclear paper featuring her handwritten lyrics and imagery. The disc sits on a foam stud on the inside cover and dried rose petals have been placed between the pages, complementing the flower imagery that features throughout.

Artist: **Vromb**
Label: **Ant-Zen**
Design: **Salt, Germany**
Illustration: **Logo: Bio-z (Boulay-Girard)**
Photography: **Logo: Bio-z (Boulay-Girard)**

Episode

This ambient, electronic Vromb album Episodes comes with a CD and 5-inch vinyl version, which is very rare. This music is based on a 1958 experiment on the human brain, carried out by scientist Heurel Gaudot. The design echoes this, using imagery of a plug and a TV that dates back to the 50s. The tin is made of aluminum, which was laser-cut and bent into shape. Screen-printing with a black-gloss ink applied the band's logo to the lid. The accompanying booklet is made of 150gsm black paper and the sleeves of 300gsm black card. This is a limited-edition release that was sold worldwide via specialized experimental electronic music distributors.

Artist: **REM**
Label: **Warner Bros.**
Design: **Chris Bilheimer, USA**
Illustration: **Chris Bilheimer, Jem Cohen, and Michael Stipe of REM**
Photography: **Chris Bilheimer, Jem Cohen, and Michael Stipe**

New Adventures in Hi-Fi

This package was inspired by a photo of an old elevator, a picture of which is included at the back of the book. The die-cut diamond shape in the slipcover matches the window of the elevator, while the book cover was die-cut to match the elevator car. The idea is that as the book is slid out of the bottom, it looks like the elevator is descending.

Artist: **Compilation by Thurston Moore**
Label: **Lo Recordings**
Design: **Jon Forss for Non-Format, UK**
Photography: **Donald Christie**

Root

In 1998 Thurston Moore gave Jon Tye, label manager, a DAT of 30 one-minute guitar pieces. Jon sent each one out to a hundred musicians and visual artists, who were invited to use the guitar track as a starting point for a new piece of music or artwork. Non-Format was asked to design a package in a way that would get them noticed, hence mailing them out in vacuum-cleaner bags stuffed with fluff.

The project was originally called Seed, as each guitar piece was intended as a starting point from which something else could grow, but Jon Forss suggested Root which conveyed the sense of having to search about in the bag to get at its contents. Forss laid out the text in a way that made the bags seem like actual vacuum-cleaner bags at first glance. The bags were then screen-printed and stuffed with Kapok to suggest dust. This call for entries generated enough material to produce a CD, a triple vinyl

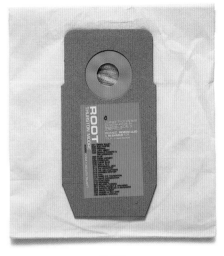

box set, and an art exhibition. Most of the CDs were produced in a jewel case but a limited edition was packaged in another vacuum-cleaner bag. The booklet with track details and images of some of the art that appeared in the exhibition was housed in a "teabag" sleeve, a textured cloth CD bag, alluding to the filter in a vacuum cleaner.

The disc itself carries a color photograph of dust which was created by emptying a vacuum-cleaner bag directly on to a scanner. Eurostile typeface was used throughout, inspired by an old upright Hoover with the font running up the side.

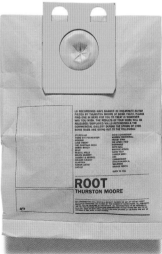

Artists: Oliver Zahle, Jens Korse, and Lars le Dous
Label: EMI / Medley
Design: Jan Nielsen, Ole Lund, Jesper Jans, and Tobias Rosenberg for 2GD, Denmark
Illustration: Jan Nielsen, Ole Lund, Jesper Jans, Soeren Nielsen, Morgan and Morell

Selvsving

Selvsving is a satirical Sunday program on a national Danish radio station produced by Oliver Zahle, Jens Korse, and Lars le Dous. To accompany the double CD release of the show's sketches, 2GD was asked to visualize the "universe" that exists around the program in the form of a book. Selvsving's staff developed a number of songs especially for the release. Together the two CDs of sketches and songs and the accompanying illustrative material provide a unique insight into the creative process of this radio program, from ideas to reality. The package is 100 percent recycled paper and, when closed, die-cuts in the cover—designed to look like a radio—allow the consumer to use one of the discs like a radio tuning dial.

Artists: **Various**
Label: **A.P.C. Section Musicale**
Design: **Rik Bas Backer, France**
Art Direction: **Pierre Bailly**
Photography: **Pierre Bailly**

Listen to This Picture

This is a compilation that came about after photographer Pierre Bailly asked a number of iconic women—including Kate Moss, Marianne Faithful, and Liv Tyler—to listen to their favorite song while he photographed them. These songs were then put together on a CD housed in this book, designed by Rik Bas Backer (see also p95 and p124). The book contains Bailly's photographs of the women and a handwritten message from them all. It was released on fashion house A.P.C.'s label Section Musicale and is sold in its stores. The design is minimal, in keeping with A.P.C.'s general style; Courier typeface was used throughout.

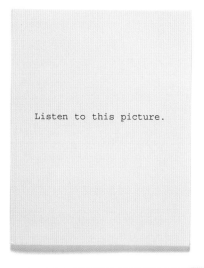

Artists: **Various**
Label: **Bremsstrahlung**
Recordings, San Diego
Design: **Richard Chartier, USA**
Illustration: **Carmen Resendez**
Photography: **Carmen Resendez**

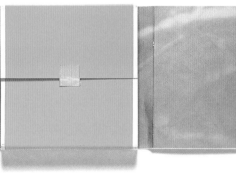

Lowercase

For this release, Richard Chartier created a five-panel card case which allows for the inclusion of four CDs and 30 information cards. Originally the inserts were printed in silver on a flysheet, but the paper did not hold the metallic ink well and created a lot of bleed. They then tried Cougar Opaque stock, which took the metallic ink better, and Tyvek® sleeves to hold two of the CDs. Two further CDs of the same music were also included, housed in a separate envelope. The idea is that the owner shares the CDs out, offering something

unexpected and expanding the impact. "I wonder how many people did this," says Chartier. "And also if the people who just got the 'friend' CDs were enticed to buy the complete package, and then if they passed on the 'friend' CDs?"

Chartier used card inserts rather than a booklet as he preferred the physical nature of a stack of cards. The listener is then free to reconfigure the order of them. It also gives each artist their own space, whether it be used for a short biography or a list of other releases.

The outer cover is a series of close-up photographs of textures in nature, reflecting the exploration of sounds that make up the music on the CD.

Artist: **Venetian Snares**
Label: **Hymen Records**
Design: **Salt for bombthedot,**
Germany
Photography: **Salt for bombthedot**

A Giant Alien Force

The picture viewer included in this CD package is recognized by most as either a children's toy or a tourist gift dating back to the 70s. The idea came after Stefan Alt talked with members of the band about the music on this album. They imagined it as a soundtrack for a science fiction movie about a giant alien force capturing planet earth. The images on this picture viewer visualize this invasion and were taken by Alt in various locations including New York, Missouri, Texas, Oklahoma, Arizona, and California. "We wanted to have a link between the movie medium and the music," explains Alt. "As it wasn't possible to realize the science fiction movie for real, we went for this picture medium. We tried to create an audio and visual object with artwork that would surprise the listener as well as create the mood of the 'soundtrack'." Solid Arial Black typeface was used throughout with all typography done in Illustrator and then placed onto the images using Photoshop.

Artist: **Ultra-red**
Label: **Beta Bodega Coalition,**
 Miami / Manchester / Tokyo
Design: **La Mano Fria for PL3x**
Illustration: **La Mano Fria for PL3x**
Photography: **La Mano Fria for PL3x**

Desavrollos Sostenibles (this page)
Frente 57 (top right)
**Psychological Operations in
Guerrilla Warfare** (bottom right)
Steven Castro founded the Beta Bodega
Coalition in 1998. The label mixes
underground electronic music with
politics, described by Castro as abstract
electronic activism. Each release is
accompanied by rigorous manifestos
regarding US foreign policy in Panama,
Columbia, and Cuba among others.
Shown here is the packaging for two
albums on the Beta Bodega label and
one on the sub-label Rice and Beans.

The label's aim is for everything produced
to relate directly to Latino culture. Rice
and beans are the staple diet in South
America and Bodega means corner-store
in the Latino neighborhoods of New York
and Miami, where many products from
that neighborhood's country of origin can
be found. The colors used in the packages
are from generic Latin products and the
imagery revisits many of Latin America's
struggles over the last century.
The designer intends the enclosed
wraparound information poster to be read
and put on the wall, and for the mailing
cards to be returned to the label. This
is a label with a strong message which
aims to extend the experience far
beyond the music.

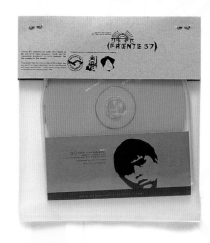

Artist:	**REM**
Label:	**Warner Bros.**
Design:	**Michael Stipe of REM and Chris Bilheimer, USA**
Illustration:	**Chris Bilheimer, Brook Dillon**
Photography:	**Chris Bilheimer, Brook Dillon**

Up

REM's Up album cover takes its inspiration from the corrugated packaging of a box of cookies, with its diamond-patterned design.

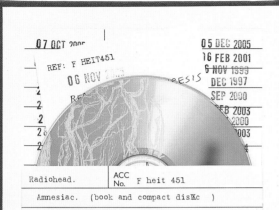

07 OCT 2005

REF: F HEIT451

06 NOV 2005

05 DEC 2005
16 FEB 2001
6 NOV 1999
DEC 1997
SEP 2000

Radiohead.

ACC No. F heit 451

Amnesiac. (book and compact disc)

NOSUCH LIBRARY
MITHRAS TAUROCTONOS

Catachresis College

LIBRARY

This book is to be hidden.
Labyrinthine structures are entered at the reader's own risk.
Nosuch Library and Lending Service cannot be held responsible for Misuse.

AMNESIAC

RADIOHEAD

2001

Artist: **Radiohead**
Label: **Parlophone**
Design: **Stanley Donwood, UK**
Illustration: **Stanley Donwood and Radiohead**
Photography: **Stanley Donwood and Radiohead**

Amnesiac

Stanley Donwood created this book which also contains Radiohead's Amnesiac CD, produced by specialist printer Artomatic. Donwood had the book cloth-bound with a library borrowing card slot printed on the inside cover. "It's supposed to be like an old book of slightly eccentric research that would be found hidden in a locked drawer in a dusty attic in a haunted house," explains Donwood. "It's a sort of a diary or a journal of someone living alone and unloved in London." Donwood and members of Radiohead, who were heavily involved in the project, created the illustrations that run throughout the book.

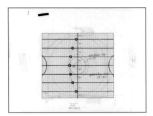
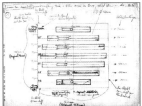
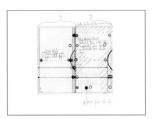

Artist: **Vienna Art Orchestra**
Label: **Verve / Amadeo / Polygram**
Packaged
Edition: **Elisabeth Kopf and the Vienna Art Orchestra**
Design: **Elisabeth Kopf, Austria**
Box Music &
Composition: **Martin Zrost**

Little Orchestra

This music box was designed and created to celebrate the Vienna Art Orchestra's 20th Anniversary. Kopf was asked to design a package for 30 special editions of the CD. There were no restrictions other than the budget. The box comprises three jazz-based CDs with music ranging from subtle ballads to big-band jazz. "My plan was to create a packaging portrait of the Vienna Art Orchestra and something to celebrate its 20th anniversary," explains Kopf. "The other main idea was to show a little bit of what was inside the package: music. The key question was how to show music? I didn't want to write about it, or just show pictures of the musicians, so I figured, it had to make music."

Kopf developed a mechanical process using the air flow produced on opening and closing the box to create musical sounds. She drilled a pattern of holes into the cases, that led the air through little brass components, causing tiny plates to vibrate, producing sound. The position of the holes allows control over the timing of the vibrations (rhythm and melody) and the size of the brass plates determines the tone and pitch.

Each box was handmade. "The advantage of this packaging is the magic of how it functions," comments Kopf. "It not only covers music, it also makes music. By simply opening or closing this packaging

it attracts the attention of every ear in the room, it amuses and it amazes people, everybody loves to play with it." The box is made of Plexiglas and all text (in Avenir typeface) was engraved onto its spine. Each box plays its own tune; all 30 together comprise a full orchestral composition. The music of this Little Orchestra has been recorded and produced as a CD in its own right.

Artists: **Various**
Label: **Spezialmaterial**
Design: **Christof Steinmann,**
Switzerland

Spezialmaterial Box

This wooden box contains seven CDs and a booklet and was created for Swiss label Spezialmaterial—a collective of visual designers and artists, producers, musicians, and DJs. It was designed to represent the label's work in the competition for music funding from the city and district of Lucerne. The box is made from MDF and the CDs are housed in simple jewel cases with self-adhesive CD-labels. The middle of the sticker that is not meant to be used on the disc itself, has been stuck on the outside of the jewel case, to complete the image on each cover.

A booklet explains how the label functions, it also presents details of the artists' biographies, a history of the label, its network across Europe, and an overview of the label's flyers, posters, and stage visuals. Spezialmaterial was eventually awarded with funding that allowed the label to continue to publish music on a regular basis. Only seven of these boxes were produced.

Artist: Hard Sleeper
Label: Émigré Music
Design: Peter Maybury,
Ireland and USA

Dreaming Out Loudest

In 1994 US label Émigré produced a compilation CD entitled Dreaming Out Loudest. The music was instrumental and thought of as music to dream to, hence the design of the boxes featuring feather images—the type that pillows are filled with. For the first release, a miniature handmade pillow was enclosed along with the CD, plus a small booklet with stories about sleepwalking. In order to keep the cost per box down Rudy VanderLans, head of the Émigré label, produced many more boxes than were needed which inspired him to extend the idea by turning it into a series.

The third release in the series (shown here) was designed by Peter Maybury. A 72-page booklet accompanies the release featuring French-folded pages with photographs taken by Maybury mainly while travelling on a train in China. These have been interspersed with images and graphic elements from other sources, to suggest a non-linear and slightly dream-like journey. The French fold was initially thought of purely to avoid show-through, but it also softens the book, and Maybury now believes it also influences how one feels about the images.

Artist: **The Cooper Temple Clause**
Label: **Morning Records**
Design: **Richard Andrews**
for BMG, UK
Photography:**Richard Andrews**
and Paul Donohue

See This Through and Leave

The Cooper Temple Clause hails from Reading in the UK—also the location of the photo shoot for imagery used in this promotional release of the band's album, See This Through and Leave. Designer Richard Andrews based the whole album, single, and promotional campaign for the band on the idea of the "middle-England family", particularly what the band see as a suffocating life in Reading. Working together, Andrews and Paul Donohue looked for subtle references to middle-England life when doing the shoot. Andrews then placed the resulting photographs in this specially produced gold foil-blocked photograph album, which is foam-padded front and back and sealed by mock leather plastic.

"I needed an idea where people could familiarize with the theme involved in the campaign—family," explains Andrews. "The photo album did just that. By making it look really cheap it also set the tone for the type of lifestyle I was trying to portray. It takes all the ideas behind the campaign and reinforces them on a three-dimensional level." This package won Andrews a UK CAD award in 2002 for Best Special Packaging.

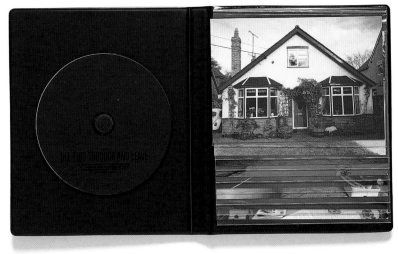

Artist: **Kpist**
Label: **NONS / MNW**
Design: **Sweden Graphics, Sweden**
Illustration: **Sweden Graphics**
Photography: **Sweden Graphics**

Golden Coat

Each of these CDs for Kpist has been personalized with gold spray, making each one unique. Inspired by the title Golden Coat, designers at Sweden Graphics donned overalls and spent four hours in a garage spraying each one of the 2000 print run. Firecracker typeface, designed by Sweden Graphics, was used throughout.

Artist: **Frou Frou**
Label: **Island Records**
Design: **Michael Nash Associates, UK**

Breathe In and Details

This is one of 200 promo releases of electronic pop act Frou Frou's Breathe In single and Details album. Once the PVC slipcase is removed the viewer is faced with two sheets of plastic. The first is a blank sheet with the instructions "breathe on" in the corner. Warm breath makes heat-sensitive ink letters visible, forming lyrics from the album. The second sheet is visibly printed with lyrics but these need to be read through the enclosed eyeglass. The Frou Frou typeface was created for the title; other copy is set in Avante Garde. To fit with the electronic music the package is functional and minimalist. Its size, format, and attention to detail make it a highly desirable and collectable piece.

Artist: **Quinoline Yellow**
Label: **skam recordings**
Design: **bhatoptics, UK**

LMW

Skam Recordings is respected as much for the quality of the underground electronic music on its releases as for the packaging that they come in, and this one, for musician Quinoline Yellow, is no exception. The whole album package, entitled LMW, is based on the idea of motoring, and sees a conventional tax disc holder being used to house the 3-inch CD. An inserted card that carries artist and record label details also has a black and white image of a BMW on it. Each release has an individual number plate giving it a unique code that the consumer can register on the LMW website. On the inside of the cover is the artist title in Grade 2 Braille, which is a trademark of skam releases. The green / blue-tinted sun-visor edging on the plastic, and specially designed key rings and air fresheners add to this motoring-inspired CD packaging.

Artists: **Various**
Label: **Nuphonic**
Design: **Ora-Íto, Italy**

CAP One

Cappellini plan to release a whole series of music CDs in partnership with the independent London recording house Nuphonic. Play with the Cappellini Family is the first of the collaborations. Chosen by Nuphonic's artistic director David Hill and Giulio Cappellini, the tracks on the CD are varied in terms of sound, rhythm, style, and influence; there is no apparent common denominator.

The CD packaging was designed by Ora-Íto, the creator of previous Cappellini advertising campaigns, and is in line with Cappellini's philosophy—in which every product has an equal secondary role of being a vehicle of communication for the company. The design is based on the idea of the Toy Box that the company released in 2001. Inside the boxed CD package is a booklet containing many Cappellini products, including Marc Newson's slump table and Tom Dixon's S chair, as well as an airfix model-type frame containing plastic models of furniture that the consumer can put together at home.

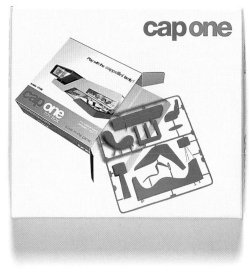

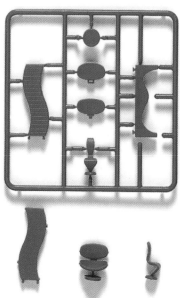

"I think we'll see that the rise in the electronic distribution of music sparks a new interest in the possibilities that physical packaging can offer"

Chris Murphy, Fällt

Fällt publishes music digitally as well as in CD format. Chris Murphy founded the company in the mid-90s and has worked with designers including Tina Frank (Mego), Angela Lorenz (Ritornell / Staalplaat), Taylor Dupree (12k), and Richard Chartier (LINE / Intrasitive).

Many of the major record labels claim to be losing profits because of illegal free downloading of music from the Internet. What do you think can be done to regulate this and do you think people should be charged for it?

The major labels deserve to be in the position they're in. More often than not, they've postponed decisions about moving their work online and hampered most attempts to do so by others whether legitimate or otherwise. They have lacked leadership and it's no surprise that we're currently in a situation where no clear technical standard exists. As well as MP3, other formats are being discussed—including digital rights management—but these all infringe upon an individual's right to move music they have legitimately bought from one platform to another. If I buy a CD I have the right to rip its contents to listen to on my iPod, yet several of the larger labels are pressing for this right to be stripped away, so that the end user has to buy multiple formats of the same content. I feel this is wrong and there's no question that the attitude of the major labels is alienating consumers.

I think a charge of some description for music is only fair, but the figures being proposed by the major labels are absurd. A software product costs far less to produce than its hardware equivalent, and pricing should reflect this. Perhaps a move towards enabling micro-payments will revolutionize our attitude towards payment for music and other forms of content, making us more willing to pay for it.

Can you really see MP3 taking over?

What we're interested in exploring at Fällt is blurring the boundaries between the software and hardware approaches. I think it's a mistake to talk about electronically distributed music as replacing physically distributed music. There are so many things that can't be achieved on screen: embossing, die-cutting, creative folding, the look, and feel of different types of paper.

What are the implications if it does take over in so far as the possible loss of the album cover that over the years has become a major social document?

I honestly can't envision a time when physical aspects of packaging no longer exist. More likely is when the majority of design is electronically distributed or accessed, and the physical product becomes more specialist orientated. My major concern about this is the way in which purely digital files have a habit of being superseded by developments and fluctuations within the software market. Just imagine a time when all your carefully collected and painstakingly preserved digital covers are lost as a result of the relentless drive to upgrade software: The file 'david_bowie_heroes_artwork' cannot be opened because the program that created it could not be found.

Ireland, 2002

"I think people will always buy CDs,
there's nothing like having the real thing"

The Client: Alison Fielding, Beggars Group

Alison Fielding is art director of the highly successful, UK record label Beggars Group which incorporates 4AD, Mowax, Mantra Recordings, Beggars Banquet, and XL Recordings. She has been working in the music industry for over ten years, art directing covers for many bands including The Prodigy, The Charlatans, Six by Seven, and Natacha Atlas.

How important do you think the album cover is?
In the past, the album cover has reflected both cultural and political changes of the time and it has always been an area of design where there has been freedom of visual expression.

What do you most enjoy about designing a cover?
Each project is unique and it is often inspiring to work with different photographers and illustrators, as well as with the bands who usually have an idea or two themselves.

Are decisions about covers based on the marketability of it rather than the design aesthetic?
Very rarely, unless it was a completely offensive or unsuitable cover.

What are the disadvantages of the conventional jewel case?
I think on an aesthetic level the design often loses a lot when jewel cases are used, unfortunately though for designers practical factors often outweigh the aesthetic ones.

Do you think there is enough creativity within CD cover design?
I think design for the music industry sees some of the most experimental and exciting graphic design around, but also some of the worst. However, whenever there are clients involved then there are always going to be restraints on budget, taste, and so on.

Will the real thing lose out to MP3?
Possibly, but I think people will always buy CDs, there's nothing like having the real thing.

London, 2002

Downloadable Artwork

"Content is king in today's digital age, and good innovative design can play a huge part in making content relevant and engaging to different audiences."

Rob King, EMI Studios Group

Artist: **Thievery Corporation**
Label: **Eighteenth Street**
Design: **Neal Ashby and Matthew Curry for Ashby Design, USA**
Illustration: **Neal Ashby and Matthew Curry**

Versions

Ashby and electronic music artists Thievery Corporation have collaborated for over eight years creating Grammy®-nominated music packaging. Inspired by a shared appreciation of The Beatles Revolver album cover by Klaus Voorman, Ashby and Curry tried their hand at a true collaboration for the package design of Thievery Corporation's recent release, Versions, eventually creating a 32-page illustrated book for the package. Once finished, Ashby and Curry decided to tell the story about the three-month process that led to final product, the result of which was a case study website called The Art of Versions. "The idea of the site was not only to walk viewers through the process that created art from over 300 individual sources," explains Ashby, "but also to look ahead to the emerging iPod age, where music packaging will turn to an all-digital format. We did this by taking the static pieces of art, and the environment that we had created with them, and bringing them to life." The designers wanted to create a sense of depth within the site and achieved this by using complementary tools. "Once our interface was designed, we began breaking down items and graphics in Photoshop, making sure the raster images were saved out as transparent PNGs so that each layer would properly interact with the other," explains Curry. "Once all the graphics were saved out accordingly, we began rebuilding the interface using several different Flash files to properly render the depth of layering we wanted to create." To date, the Art of Versions site has received over two million hits worldwide.

01 **ashbydesign**
02 portfolio
03 studio profile
04 news
05 contact

ashby design provides consultancy across a spectrum of design disciplines. our portfolio includes music packaging, corporate identities, annual reports, brochures, book and magazine design and interactive media. our clients are large and small, encompassing a wide range of industries. design solutions begin with an idea rather than a template. we strive to create work that not only poses a question, but in the same breath answers that question as well. work that has a respect for the past, yet looks forward. work that has poetry.

Artist: **The Enemy**
Label: **Warner**
Art Direction and Design:
Gerard Saint, Richard Andrews, and Markus Karlsson for Big Active

We'll Live And Die In These Towns

Shown here are images of the interactive packaging created by Big Active for the release of The Enemy's album We'll Live And Die In These Towns. The packaging can only be accessed when the complete album bundle is bought through iTunes. "Our idea for the physical formats and the campaign itself was based upon the metaphor of a railway departure board—as a way of imparting different messages within a really succinct visual format—and giving the campaign a really strong identity," explains Saint. "Obviously the online and digital formats give us the chance to develop the idea naturally using animation to bring the idea to life." The artwork was built from photographs of the departure board at Liverpool Street Station in London. The designers then reconstructed this digitally to create a basic model from which to assemble the necessary different versions.

There is a digital version of the album, available online through iTunes, which uses the idea of the signboard changing destination each time a new track is played. In addition, the signboard is animated for online advertising, and there is a customizable version on the band's website. "Work like this sets a precedent for how digital formatting and physical formatting can be integrated to play to each other's strengths while creating a clear identity for the release that's inspiring and strong enough to translate well across all media," adds Saint.

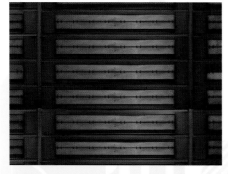

Artist: **Beck**
Label: **Interscope Records**
Art Direction and Design:
Gerard Saint and Mat Maitland for Big Active

The Information

Interactive digital packaging is one way in which designers can encourage buyers to download albums rather than buy single tracks. Big Active's packaging for Beck's <u>The Information</u> is a great example. It can only be accessed when the complete album bundle is bought through iTunes or other online retailers. As Gerard Saint of Big Active explains, "The idea was based upon our concept for the physical album packaging, which involved stickers so that the listener can create their own sleeve or customize their CD package. The interactive packaging moves this idea into a digital format so that you can play with the imagery in a similar way on your computer." Several websites were created so that fans could upload their designs. Artwork for the album was created by, among others, Jody Barton, Estelle, David Foldvari, Genevieve Gauckler, Michael Gillette, and Jasper Goodall.

Artist: **3cycle**
Label: **Self-released**
Design: **Alexander Egger / Satellites Mistaken for Stars, Austria**

3 x 3 Tracks

Egger created these wallpapers and screensavers for the album launch of blues band Tricycle. The band plays a simple electrified version of blues, reduced and open, with a strong basis in traditional delta blues enhanced with modern European elements. "The elemental structures of blues are transformed into a very basic and reduced design using the typical wires of Viennese tramways for the basis of the design," explains Egger. "The wires are not used in a conventional way as authentic photographs, but in a stylized, open way." The wallpapers and screensavers were used as a simple yet effective promotional tool and were downloadable free on the band's website. Web-related downloads are not something one would typically relate to blues bands—it is an innovative idea within the genre.

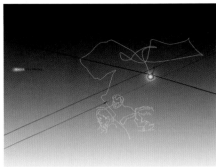

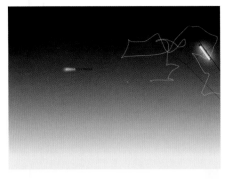

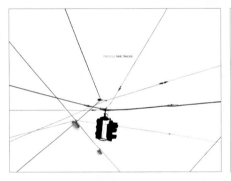

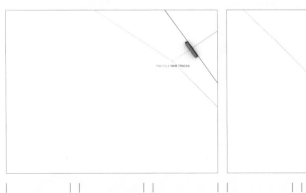

Artist: **God Bless the Aircondition**
Label: **Self-released**
Design: **Alexander Egger / Satellites
Mistaken for Stars, Austria**

Flags Disturb
the Atmosphere

Egger created these wallpapers and screen savers as part of an integrated visual concept for the indie band God Bless the Aircondition, containing CD artwork, concert visuals, website, and posters. The concept for the artwork was to play in a poetic and subtle way with rough deconstructed industrial elements to reflect the sound of the band—eruptive instrumental and emotive melody. "The idea was to dissect and reflect on urbanism, consumerism, technology, and mass culture to come up with a transient, fragile, and poetical use of these raw materials," explains Egger. "This has been interpreted with hand-drawn elements inspired by film noir, city riots, and political manifestos from South America." The wallpapers and screen savers were made available as free downloads on the band's website.

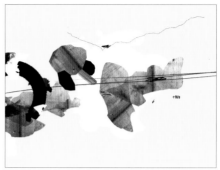

Artist: **Mutya Buena**
Label: **Universal / Island**
Design: **Abbey Road Interactive, UK**

Real Girl

Shown here is an interactive booklet created for the e-Deluxe version of Mutya Buena's debut album. The booklet is available with the album when purchased from digital music retailers such as iTunes. It is based on an extension of the physical album artwork and includes lyrics, credits, biography, links to artist websites and third-party sites, and photographs. It works as a downloadable interactive book. These booklets certainly enrich the user experience by giving them something to look through when they purchase the album, including press imagery that is not included in the physical package.

Picture used with kind permission of Universal Island Records Limited.

Artist:	**Mika**
Label:	**Island**
Design:	**Airside / Mika / Da Wack, UK**

Life in Cartoon Motion

Airside worked closely with Mika to develop the creative and visual identity for the release of his first album, Life in Cartoon Motion. Mika and his sister, artist Da Wack (Yasmine), had already created characters for Mika's visuals. "We took the elements and characters Yasmine had created, added to them, then collaborated with Mika and Yasmine to complete the 'Mika world,'" explains Anne Brassier of Airside. Shown here are stills of a short web animation developed to promote Mika's first single Relax.

Artist: **God Bless the Aircondition**
Label: **Self-released**
Design: **Alexander Egger / Satellites**
              Mistaken for Stars, Austria

A Day Out

Shown here is A Day Out, a promo application given away free through the band's website to coincide with the release of the album Flags Disturb the Atmosphere (see p161). It consists of a forest through which the viewer can navigate by using computer keyboard arrows. Depending on their position in the forest, the viewer can hear one of the soundtraces (three different instruments: bass, guitar, drums) of an instrumental audio track. The user can find the position at which they can hear all three tracks running parallel in the mix, or search for a position at which just one track is playing. "The aim is for it to feel like the viewer is walking through a forest, hearing birds sing, and realizing that there is something else, a sound, firstly very quietly in the distance, something which doesn't fit with the normal noises in a forest," explains Egger. "The application is meant to be a playful way to bring the audience closer to the sound of the band and create a certain mystic atmosphere around it. The application was part of the enhanced CD-extra and also available as a download on the band's website.

Walking, breathing. Don't force yourself too much. Sometimes a song passes by. Things happen. Every day. Choose to stay in things or not, get confused and wonder why. Find your own sound. Forget. Try again.

 Use your arrow keys to navigate.

You never know if you have given yourself enough time to get it all.

Enter the forest.

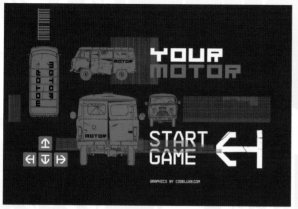

Artist:	Motor
Label:	Mute U.S.
Design:	Hugo Göldner for Codeluxe, UK / Germany
Programming:	Oliver Greschke

Klunk

This Flash game was produced for the album release of the electronic duo Motor, and contains three levels full of exploding cars, aircrafts, and other objects. The idea is for the graphics within the game to correspond with the sound of the artists' music—rough, dirty, and loud. "The story of the game is that the player is on their way to the next Motor gig and needs to avoid hitting other vehicles on the highway," explains Göldner. "Fortunately, the famous Neubauwelt book was released at the same time, so we used the objects and disturbed them to make the cars look old and dirty." The game was promoted on the Motor website (din9.com) during the release of the band's album.

Artist: **Keane**
Label: **Interscope Records**
Art Direction and Design:
      Gerard Saint and Richard
      Andrews for Big Active
Illustration: **Sanna Annukka**

Under the Iron Sea

For the release of Keane's <u>Under the Iron Sea</u>, Big Active was commissioned to "create a symbolic approach to the design." In order to establish the campaign with a clearly defined identity, Big Active worked with Annukka to create a strong visual narrative for the album. "The artwork is seemingly innocent in feel, but with an underlying twist of menace reflecting a darker, more topical lyrical mood," explains Saint. The CD was designed to maximize the use of a roll-fold booklet inserted on its side; this unfolds vertically to reveal another world beneath the cover's turbulent waves. A hardbacked "storybook" format housed the DVD version of the album. A series of mini scenarios were developed as images for subsequent single releases, and were used to create the downloadable wallpapers, shown here, that were made available to fans on Keane's website.

Artist: **Bonobo**
Label: **Ninja Tune**
Design: **Ed Templeton**
          for Red Design, UK

Days to Come

Red Design was originally commissioned simply to create the album artwork for Bonobo's <u>Days to Come</u>, but ended up adding an animated web promo. "It was something that happened on the day... While on the shoot for the album artwork, we realized the image we were shooting could make a great stop-motion animation," explains Templeton. "We decided to go ahead and make the animation and then persuade the artist's label, ninjatune, to use it as an e-card and online ad for the album." The imagery used for the album artwork, and within the animation, was created using items the designers found in Bonobo's flat. "We wanted to create an alternative portrait of Bonobo for the album cover so we raided his flat and took everything we could find that was light colored, and made physical collages from these found items in a local wood."

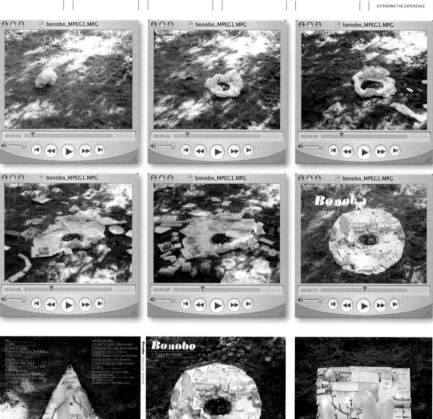

"If people just want the music they will buy the MP3, but if they want the package ... they will buy into the object."

David Lane

David Lane is an art director and designer. After graduating from Central Saint Martins College of Art and Design, London, he set up a small studio where he now works. He also freelances for a number of other studios including Multistorey and Wolff Olins. He has designed record covers for Gossip, Noisettes, Dega Breaks, and Tronik Youth. His clients include Backyard Records, Mercury Music, CSDK, The Bastion Host Gallery, and Boxfresh. His work has been published in Grafik, Creative Review, Design Week, and Computer Arts magazine.

What do you think the future holds for music packaging now that so much music is downloaded?
I think the music industry needs to realize that cutting the price and production quality of music packaging is not the answer. Downloads will always win the price war, but they can never be a desirable, collectible object. Downloads are fantastic, but people inherently like objects. I will never get rid of my record collection, partly because on the right equipment they sound better, but also because I have lots of 12in artworks that mean as much to me as the music that they contain. I think there is a really strong argument to make music packaging more exciting, and for the industry to spend more on producing fewer, high-quality items. If people just want the music, they will buy the MP3, but if they want the package and they are willing to spend a little more on it, they will buy in to the object. It is similar to the choice between buying a first-edition hardback book to take pride of place on your bookshelf, or buying a cheap softback reprint to read on a long train journey and lend to a friend, never to be seen again. I think it is an interesting time for music packaging, and potentially quite an exciting one. Ultimately, it is up to the record companies—hopefully they will listen to their heart and not their accountants.

How do you think the role of the graphic designer might change because of this?
I think that designers will have to consider the routes of screen and print as two very different things. To date, when you buy an MP3, you simply get the graphic from the CD single, maybe slightly altered, but only so it still looks good at smaller sizes. I think in the future there will certainly be scope for designs to stop being static, not to become a promo, but to occupy the area in between music video, interactive media, and still artwork. Hopefully there is a way for this to happen without taking on the flash or web aesthetic, but we shall see. In print, I think people will really have to consider the whole object and not just produce an artwork to be pasted on to a number of formats.

What can designers do to move with the "digital times"?
I think there is really scope for interactivity and motion, though it is a problem to achieve this without sacrificing a static image's bold statement and memorability. Often, when becoming interactive, they rely on gimmicks, such as those used in DVD intro menus. I think I have yet to see one that does justice to the movie it is navigating.

Rather than mourning the death of physical music packaging, should we instead celebrate the arrival of a whole new image / music format?
Yes I think we should embrace the arrival of a new format and I won't believe physical music packaging is dead until it happens. DJs and collectors still buy records, and fans still buy band merchandise. I really don't think true fans will be satisfied with a 72dpi thumbnail as a record of their purchase.

"The word 'packaging' will take on other meanings. Physical packaging will become digital."

The Client: Rob King, EMI Studios Group

Rob King has worked extensively in both the media and music industries since the late 1990s. Between 2001 and 2003 he was part of the management team at lastminute.com. He went on to work for a global communications agency. He joined EMI Studios Group as Business Development Manager in 2007.

CD packages are great examples of some of the most innovative and experimental graphic design today. Why do you think this is?
CDs are mainstream creative delivery platforms. Therefore designers are challenged with some amazing briefs in order to support the artist and have as much impact as possible when the product is released.

What part do you think designers can play in keeping people interested in buying CD packages rather than just downloading them?
For the serious collector, they can play a huge part. People who enjoy CD box sets will always enjoy purchasing special editions and limited-release titles. However, for the mass market, it is becoming increasingly difficult to maintain current sales levels in CDs. Unfortunately good design is not going to change that; the problem is fundamentally related to changing trends, such as people using the Internet more in every aspect of daily life.

What do you think the future holds for music packaging now that so much music is downloaded?
The word "packaging" will take on other meanings. Physical packaging will become digital and the opportunities for design will change. We are starting to see the early forms of digital music packaging, but I think it's the tip of the iceberg. As more music is bought online, inevitably content and intellectual property rights owners will create new and interesting forms of "packaging."

How do you think the role of the graphic designer might change because of this?
Designers will ultimately need to be skilled in all areas of the digital design process. However, the fundamentals won't change; good design and creative ideas will continue to be the most important factors.

What can designers do to move with the "digital times" and offer buyers something other than simply a thumbnail image of an album cover when they download music?
The best thing designers can do is not be constrained by convention. There is a huge opportunity to create new design ideas relating to online music and movies / TV. We live in an age of information overload—people are having to filter the information and content they don't want from that they do, e-mails, websites, etc. Content is king in today's digital age and good innovative design can play a huge part in making content relevant and engaging to different audiences.

Rather than mourning the death of physical music packaging, should we instead celebrate the arrival of a whole new image / music format?
I think celebrating is perhaps a bit strong for now. However, I feel very strongly that mourning the death of physical packaging is totally the wrong thing to do. There is clearly still a place for physical packaging, certainly for the next 5–7 years, and I think people will need to strike a good balance between the two with physical packaging eventually becoming obsolete.

Contact Details & Acknowledgments

Contact Details

12k (Taylor Deupree)
taylor@12k.com
www.12k.com

23 (David McSherry)
www.23online.co.uk

2GD
2gd@2gd.dk
www.2gd.dk

2manydesigners
conact@2manydesigners.net
www.2manydesigners.net

4AD
www.4ad.com

Abbey Road Interactive
tom.williams@abbeyroad.com
www.abbeyroad.com

A-Side Studio
contact@a-sidestudio.co.uk
www.a-sidestudio.co.uk

Adjective Noun
email@adjectivenoun.co.uk
www.adjectivenoun.co.uk

Airside
info@airside.co.uk
www.airside.co.uk
www.airsideshop.com

Alex Baumgardt Visuelle Kommunikation
alex@abvk.de
www.abvk.de

Amp Associates
info@ampuk.com

A.P.C Section Musicale
music@apc.fr
www.apc.fr

Apt 13 (Phillip Dwyer)
hello@apt13.com
www.apt13.com

Arkhipoff, Elisabeth
earkhipoff@noos.fr

Artomatic
info@artomatic.co.uk
www.artomatic.co.uk

Ashby Design
nashby@ashbyandassociates.com

Ata Tak
info@atatak.com
www.atatak.com

Bankerwessel
jonas@bankerwessel.com
www.bankerwessel.com

Baritski, Linda
linda.baritski@btopenworld.com

Barwick, Thomas
tom.barwick@virgin.net
www.thomasbarwick.com

Beggars Group
alisonfielding@beggars.com
www.beggars.com

bhatoptics (LMW Motors)
data@bhatoptics.com
www.bhatoptics.com

Big Active
bp@bigactive.com
www.bigactive.com

Bilheimer, Chris
crb@chronictown.com

Blur Traffic Design
info@traffic-design.com
www.traffic-design.com

Bombshelter Design
zacharylarner@bombshelterdesign.com
www.bombshelterdesign.com

bombthedot
office@bombthedot.com
www.bombthedot.com

Brilliant
frans@brilliant.nu
www.brilliant.nu/frans.html

Bucy, Moussi
m-frdl@servus.at

Burgopak
info@burgopak.com
www.burgopak.com

Büro X
christoph@interkool.com
www.interkool.com

Byram, Stephen
Steve_Byram@sonymusic.com

Byrne, David
doyle@doylepartners.com
www.doylepartners.com

Cappellini
cappellini@cappellini.it
www.cappellini.it

Carpark Records
info@carparkrecords.com
www.carparkrecords.com

Carter, Rob and Nick
www.robandnick.com

Chartier, Richard
chartier@3particles.com
www.3particles.com

Chemical Box
bureau@chemicalbox.com
www.chemicalbox.com

Codeluxe
martin@codeluxe.com
www.codeluxe.com

Crush
info@crushed.co.uk
www.crushed.co.uk

Cuttings (Sarah Littasy)
littasy@cuttings.at
www.cuttings.at
www.g-stoned.com

Donwood, Stanley
www.slowlydownward.com
www.radiohead.com

Doyle Partners
doyle@doylepartners.com
www.doylepartners.com

ehquestionmark (Boom Bip)
enquirehere@ehquestionmark.com
www.ehquestionmark.com

Eikes Grafischer Hort
info@eikesgrafischerhort.com
www.eikesgrafischerhort.com
www.hort.org.uk

EkhornForss / Non-Format
info@ekhornforss.com
www.non-format.com

Émigré
editor@emigre.com
www.emigre.com

Faith (Paul Sych)
info@faith.ca
www.faith.ca

Fällt / Fehler
chris@fallt.com
www.fallt.com/artists/fehler

Felder Grafikdesign (Peter Felder)
felder.grafik@aon.at
www.feldergrafik.at

Fetis, Laurent
info@laurentfetis.com
www.laurentfetis.com

FJD (Fujitajirodesign)
fjd@fides.dti.ne.jp
www.fjd.jp

Foo Fighters
creati4@bmg.com
www.rcarecords.com

Frank, Tina (Mego)
hello@frank.at
www.frank.at

Gauckler, Geneviève
genevieve@g2works.com
www.g2works.com

Gellender, Walker
design@walker-gellender.co.uk

Goddemeyer, Daniel
daniel@someprojects.org
www.someprojects.org

Groovisions
grv@groovisions.com
www.groovisions.com

Heads Inc.
info@headsinc.com
www.headsinc.com

Hiorthøy, Kim
kimim@online.no
www.smalltownsupersound.com
www.runegrammofon.com
www.thisisrealart.com

Hopper, Sarah
s.hopper@virgin.net

Hydrafuse
info@hydrafuse.com
www.hydrafuse.com

Ilhjalmsson, Gunnar Thor
gunnar@deluxe.is
www.deluxe.is

intr_version records
aaron@intr-version.com
www.intr-version.com

Jutojo
info@jutojo.de
www.jutojo.de

Karlssonwilker Inc.
tellmewhy@karlssonwilker.com
www.karlssonwilker.com

Kitty-Yo
raik@kitty-yo.de
www.kitty-yo.de

Klausen, Brad
brad@tenclub.net

Kopf, Elisabeth
e.kopf@netway.at

Lane, David
dave_lane@mac.com
www.davidlaneuk.com

Lorenz, Angela
info@alorenz.net
www.alorenz.net

Lsd-sign (Laurent Seroussi)
lsd_sign@club-internet.fr

Lucky Kitchen
aaland@luckykitchen.com
www.luckykitchen.com

MCA Records
www.mcarecords.com

Meat and Potatoes Inc
info@meatoes.com
www.meatoes.com

Michael Nash Associates
richard@michaelnash.co.uk
www.michaelnashassociates.com

Milk
info@milkcommunications.com
www.milkcommunications.com

MOOT Design
moot@btinternet.com
www.moot.com

Mortensen, Rune
post@runemortensen.no
www.runemortensen.no

Multifresh
ask@multifresh.com
www.multifresh.com

No Days Off
info@nodaysoff.com
www.nodaysoff.com

non recordings
meem@meem.org
www.meem.org

Ohio Girl Design and Photography
info@ohiogirl.com
www.ohiogirl.com

Output
info@studio-output.com
www.studio-output.com

Pao & Paws / Taipei, Tokyo, Shanghai, London
pao@paopaws.com
www.paopaws.com

Peter and Paul
paul@peterandpaul.co.uk
www.peterandpaul.co.uk

Peter Maybury Studio
mail@softsleeper.com
www.softsleeper.com

PL3x (Beta Bodega Coalition)
info@pl3x.com
www.pl3x.com

Planet Mu
mike@planet-mu.com
www.planet-mu.com

pleasedesign
tendency@mac.com

Public International
info@publicinternational.com
www.publicinternational.com

RCA Records
creati4@bmg.com
www.rcarecords.com

Red Design
info@red-design.co.uk
www.red-design.co.uk

Rik Bas Backer
rikbb@wanadoo.fr

Root
christopher@rootdesign.co.uk
www.rootdesign.co.uk

St. Paulus (Nicolai Schaanning Larsen)
nicolai@saintpaulus.com
www.saintpaulus.com

Sagmeister Inc.
www.sagmeister.com

Satellites Mistaken for Stars
alex@satellitesmistakenforstars.com
www.satellitesmistakenforstars.com

Seeger, Hans and John Shachter
hansseeger@earthlink.net
jshachter397@earthlink.net
www.aesthetics-usa.com

Soppcollective
contact@soppcollective.com
www.soppcollective.com

Spezialmaterial
kontakt@spezialmaterial.ch
www.spezialmaterial.ch

Smashing Pumpkins
vsa@vsapartners.com
www.vsapartners.com

Steinmann, Christof
steinmann@spezialmaterial.ch
www.spezialmaterial.ch

Stylorouge
rob@stylorouge.co.uk
www.stylorouge.co.uk

Surface
weisbeck@surface.de
www.surface.de

Sweden Graphics
hello@swedengraphics.com
www.swedengraphics.com

Tewes, Michael
michael.tewes@berlin.de

TGB Design
info@tgbdesign.com
www.tgbdesign.com

The Designers Republic Ltd
disinfo@thedesignersrepublic.com
www.thedesignersrepublic.com

tomato
info@tomato.co.uk
www.tomato.co.uk

Traffic
jeremy@traffic-design.com
www.traffic-design.com

twelve:ten
studio@twelveten.com
www.twelveten.com

v23 (Vaughn Oliver)
veetwentythree@dial.pipex.com

WA75 (Cedric Murac & Laurent Meszaros)
info@wa75.com
www.wa75.com

Walse Custom Design
henkel@walsecustomdesign.com
www.walsecustomdesign.com

Winkreative
info@winkorp.com
www.winkreative.com

Winter & Winter GmbH
info@winterandwinter.com
www.winterandwinter.com

Work in Progress
info@workinprogress.com
www.workinprogress.com

Yacht Associates
info@yachtassociates.com
www.yachtassociates.com

Zion Graphics (Ricky Tillblad)
ricky@ziongraphics.com
www.ziongraphics.com

Zip Design
info@zipdesign.co.uk
www.zipdesign.co.uk

Acknowledgments

First and foremost, a big thank you to all the designers, image-makers, and record labels who submitted work for inclusion in this book. We were not able to include everything that we received, but the time and effort taken to send the work in is greatly appreciated.

Also, in no particular order, many thanks to Rob Young at Wire magazine, Stefan Sagmeister at Sagmeister Inc., Jon Forss at Ekhornforss / Non-Format, Tim Stedman at MCA Records, Alison Fielding at the Beggars Group, Chris Thomson at Yacht Associates, Stephen Byram at Sony Music, Terry Felgate at Parlophone, Christopher Murphy at Fällt, and Rob O'Connor at Stylorouge who all gave their time to be interviewed for this book.

Thanks to Kate Shanahan at RotoVision for all her editorial support, Luke Herriot and everyone at Crush for the fantastic art direction and design, respectively, Jane Roe for her research assistance, Xavier Young, once again, for the outstanding photography, and Chris Foges whose original idea it was to write about a book about CD design and packaging.

Additional thanks to all of 2007's contributors, and to Lindy Dunlop and Simon Slater.

This book is for Mom.

Charlotte Rivers

Index

10 71
23 126
4AD 10, 82, 92, 155
13 Amp Records 66
A Certain Frank 56
A.P.C. 18, 95, 124, 139
Abandoned Pools 84
Abbey Road Interactive 162
Abrams, Dan 58
Accordance 37
Acoustic Dub Messengers 38
Adjective Noun 35
advertising 22
Aesthetics 73
.aiff 58
Airside 29, 75, 91, 163
AlasNoAxis 86
Alejandra and Aeron 50
Alorenz 36, 42, 63, 74, 121
Alt, Stefan 46, 141
Alva Noto 36
AMFM 122
Amnesiac 145
Amp Associates 57
Andrews, Richard 150, 158, 166
Annukka, Sanna 166
Ant-hology 52
Ant-Zen 46, 48, 52, 135
Antinos Records 48
Anything's Gonna Change My World 41
Apt 13 122
The Ark 51
Arkhipoff, Elisabeth 92
Armadeo 146
Arthur, Joseph 53
Artomatic 26, 69, 71, 145
Ashby Design 18, 21, 99, 157
Ashby, Neal 18, 21, 99, 157
Assereto, Cio 57
Aström, Kristofer 107
ata tak 56
Atlantic Records 10
Atmosphériques 92
Azizamusic 72

Backer, Rik Bas 18, 95, 124, 139
Bad Taste 120
Badly Drawn Boy 14
Bailly, Pierre 139
Baker, Alan 108
Banker, Jonas 107
Banker Wessel 107
Baritski, Linda 97
Barry 7 112
Barton, Jody 159

Barwick, Thomas 96
Basement Jaxx 106
Bates, Django 53
Baumgardt, Alexander 117
Bazeado 54
Be The Voice 98
BEC 104
Beck 12–14, 159
Bedingfield, Daniel 30
Beggars Group 45, 155
Bern, Alan 37
Berne, Tim 54–55
Berry Place Models 49
Best Special Packaging 32
Beta Bodega Coalition 142
bhatopics 152
Big Active 11–12, 14, 87, 106, 108, 158–59, 166
BigBlue 53
Bilheimer, Chris 33, 58, 73, 136, 144
Bio-z 135
Bip-Hop 68
Black Agitator 59
The Black Dog 102
Black, Jim 86
Black Market Music 69
Black Sifichi 102
Blake, Peter 16
Blanchette Press 73
The Blank Album 12
Block 67
Blue Note 10
Blueshift 125
Blur 82, 101
Blur: The Best of 101
BMG 150
Bodily Functions 125
Bombshelter Design 53
bombthedot 40, 46, 48, 52, 141
Bon Voyage 104
Bonobo 167
Boom Bip 28
Born in the UK 14
Bovine Life 68
Bowden, David 100
Bowen, Neil 100
Branellec, Marie 115
Brassier, Anne 163
A Breach of Etiquette 76
Breathe In 151
Bremsstrahlung Recordings 140
Brombron 42
Brooks 126
Brothers in Sound 35
Brûlé, Tyler 34
Bucy, Moussi 70
Buena, Mutya 162
Buffer für Gestaltung 45
Bulbul 70
Bull, Richard 43
Burden, Gary 10
Burford, Sam 91
Burgopak 69
Burnstein, Greg 60
Büro X 106
Burroughs, William 102
Buy Me Try Me 70
Byetone 36
Byram, Stephen 11, 26, 37, 53–55, 61
Byrne, David 74

3cycle 160
Calderley, David 14
Called Game 41
Calleth You, Cometh I 51
Cameron, Andrew 103
Candy Cane Children 100
Canoeing Instructional 89
CAP One 153
Capitol Records 52, 67
Cappellini, Giulio 153
Carlqvist, Frans 89
Carpark Records 120
Carter, Rob and Nick 97
Casablanca 163
Castro, Steven 142
Celluloid Mata 48
The Charlatans 108
Chartier, Richard 47, 140, 154
The Chemical Brothers 66

Chemistry Is What We Are 87
Chocolate Garden 85
Christmas promotional pack 33
Cima, Daniel 99
City Rockers 118
Clifford, John 74
Codeluxe 165
Cohen, Jem 136
Coke, Rob 126
Coldplay 79
Columbia Records 10
Compost Records 31
Computer Arts Projects 19
Connected 107
Connectors 112
The Cooper Temple Clause 150
Crandall, Bill 99
Cri 125
Crush 85
Cube Juice 41
Curry, Matthew 157
Cuttings 30

D&AD 12
Da Wack 163
Davies, Dominic 82
A Day Out 164
Days to Come 167
Deakin, Fred 29, 82, 91
Desavrollos Sostenibles 142
Designers Republic 10, 19, 87
Desperate Sound System Tour 59
Details 151
Deuchars, Marion 108
Deupree, Taylor 50
Deutsch, Andrew 50
Dillon, Brook 144
Dittz, Henry 10
Dixon, Tom 153
DJs 11, 31, 168
Doktor Kosmos 123–24
Donohue, Paul 150
Don't Be Afraid to Love 104
Donwood, Stanley 145
The Doors 10
Dorfmeister, Richard 30
Dos Partes 40
le Dous, Lars 138
downloading artwork 156–67
downloading music 12, 23, 154, 168–69
Doyle Partners 74
Doyle, Stephen 74
Dreaming Out Loud 132
Dreaming Out Loudest 149
Dupree, Taylor 154
Duran Duran 127
DVDs 12, 14, 168
Dwyer, Phillip 122

Earthless 49, 103
Eclectic Bob 85
Ecopak 18
EFA 03771 56
Egger, Alexander 160–61, 164
Ehlers, Ekkehard 42
ehquestionmark 28
Eigenmann, Sybille 45
Eighteenth Street 157
Eins 57
Ekhorn Forss 65, 113
Ekhorn, Kjell 112–13
Electric Satie 51
Electrostars 32
Elemental Clinch 48
Elton John 22
Emanuel, Hector 99
EMI 108, 111, 138, 169
Émigré 33, 132, 149
Empire Box 55
The Enemy 158
Die Entdeckung des Wetters 50
Entropy 65
Episode 135
ESL Music 99
ESound 108
Ethridge, Roe 116
Etiquette Recordings 76
Eva's Story 123

Exit Now 94
Extasy Records International 55, 84
Extrapool 42

4 Foot 11 55
Factory Records 10
Fällt 19, 68, 127, 154
Family is for Sharing 35
Farrow Design 10
Farrow, Mark 11
Fehler 68, 127
Felder Grafikdesign 119
Felder, Peter 119
Felgate, Terry 79
Fenstermacher, Frank 56
Fetis, Laurent 82, 92, 111
Fielding, Alison 45, 155
Fields, Scott 125
Fila Brazilia 126
File-13 94
file-sharing 22
Fischerspooner 18, 115–16
FJD (Fujita Jiro Design) 38, 98
Flags Disturb the Atmosphere 161, 164
Flora&Fauna 89
fly-through 19
Fodder 19
Foldvari, David 159
Fontaine, Brigitte 102
The Foo Fighters 118
Force Inc. 121
Forss, Jon 112–13, 137
Forty Years to Find a Voice 65
Frank, Tina 154
Frente 57 142
Frogman Records 75
Frou Frou 151
Fujita, Jiro 98
Futura 14
Futurism 82, 118
Fyra Nya Filmer and Reportage 124

2GD 138
96 Gestures 125
G-Stoned 30
Gallopo, Todd 55, 84
Garret, Malcolm 19
Gaubert, Michel 115
Gauckler, Geneviève 102, 159
Gaudot, Heurel 135
Gebhard Mathis Records 119
The Generation I Want 39
Geschmeidig 110
Get Me Off 106
Getting into Sinking 122
A Giant Alien Force 141
Gibb, Kate 66
Gigue, Live @ A-Musik 127
Gillette, Michael 159
Gillick, Liam 89
Gintare 103
Gnarls Barkley 19
Gnewikow, Jason 92, 104
God Bless the Aircondition 161, 164
Golden Coat 151
Göldner, Hugo 165
Good Bad Right Wrong 45
Goodall, Jasper 159
Gosling, John 71
Gotta Get Thru This 30
Gough, Damon 14
Graphic Therapy 14
Green Day 58, 73
Greenhornes 100
Greschke, Oliver 165
Gress, Drew 54
Gripenholm, John 123
Grohl, Dave 118
Groovisions 48, 60
Grünfeld, Thomas 87
Guilty 103
Günter, Bernhard 47

Habermacher, René 106
Hall, Dom 19
Hamaguchi, Ken 76
Happy House 41
Hard Sleeper 149
Haswell, Russell 110

Hattler 117
Heads Inc. 46
Healy, Jeremy 11
Heavy 45
Hed Kandi 100
Hendrickson, Robin 66, 118
Herbert 125
Herbert, Peter 72
Heroin 42
Hessles 45
Hidden Agenda 94
Hidden Truck 107
Highly Evolved 52
Hill, David 153
Himmelslichter 119
Hiorthay, Kim 95
Hipgnosis 78
Hirst, Damien 85
Holdsworth, Dan 104
Home Burns 98
Hopper, Sarah 66, 125
Hôtel Costes Quartre 105
Howell, Sarah 108
Huber, Rupert 30
Hudson, Cody 108
Humanistic 84
Humming Bird Feeder 50
Hummus 117
Hung, Tony 35
Hut Recordings 69
Hydrafuse 60
Hydrogen Dukebox 32, 70, 102
Hyman, Todd 120
Hymen Records 141

I Wish You Could Be Here With Me 111
Ichifuru, Masashi 75
If I Was Prince 75
Ignore the Beat 124
Ikeda, Ryoji 74
Impotent Fury 29, 91
In Between 31
In Through the Out Door 10
Independent Project Press 33
The Information 12, 159
Inoue, Tetsu 50
Internet 19, 21–22, 172–73
Interscope Records 159, 166
Intransitive 154
Intro 10
intr_version records 65
iPod 19, 154
Island 101, 108, 151, 162
iTunes 19, 21

Jade Tree 92
Jans, Jesper 138
Jazzanova 31
Jazzkammer 122
jbo 90
Jesus Christ Bobby 120
jewel case 14, 17–18, 20, 24, 26, 129, 155
Jirku, Tomas 65
Jump On Board, Take a Ride 111
Just a Little Bit 134
Jutojo 31
JVC 92

12k 58, 154
Kaji, Hideki 92, 111
Karlsson, Hjalti 52, 67
Karlsson, Markus 158
Karlssonwilker Inc. 52, 64, 117, 125
The Karma Collection 57
Katz, Alex 111
Keane 12, 166
Kedgley, Jason 90
Kekeland 102
Kidney, Rob 106
Kilroe, Brett 66, 118
King Louis 39
King, Rob 169
Kitchen Works 75
Kitty-Yo 84
Klausen, Brad 49
Klucevsek, Guy 37
Klunk 165
Komet 36, 68
Komiyama, Hideaki 75